THE NEW TESTAMENT OF
HIGHER BUDDHISM

THE NEW TESTAMENT

OF

HIGHER BUDDHISM

BY

TIMOTHY RICHARD, D.D., Litt.D.

ENGLISH BAPTIST MISSION, CHINA

EDINBURGH: T. & T. CLARK, 38 GEORGE STREET

1910

Printed by
MORRISON & GIBB LIMITED,

FOR

T. & T. CLARK, EDINBURGH.

LONDON : SIMPKIN, MARSHALL, HAMILTON, KENT, AND CO. LIMITED.

NEW YORK : CHARLES SCRIBNER'S SONS.

CONTENTS

I

GENERAL INTRODUCTION

II

INTRODUCTION TO THE AWAKENING OF FAITH

III

IV

V

CONTENTS

THE LOTUS SCRIPTURE ESSENCE

CHAP.   PAGE
    I. INTRODUCTORY 159
    II. THE ART OF SAVING THE WORLD . . 166
    III. ALLEGORIES 170
    IV. FAITH [BASED ON FATHERHOOD] . . . 173
    V. MEDICINAL PARABLES 174
    VI. THE RECORD OF THE MESSAGE . . . 176
    VII. PARABLE OF THE ETERNAL CITY . . . 178
    VIII. [THE FIVE HUNDRED DISCIPLES] . . 180
    IX. THE SIMPLE MADE WISE 182
    X. THE SPIRITUAL GUIDE 183
    XI. GOD'S DWELLING-PLACE—PAGODA . . 189
    XII. THE CONVERTED PERSECUTOR . . . 193
    XIII. "HOLD FAST" 197
    XIV. PEACE AND JOY 200
    XV. RESURRECTION AND NEW LIFE . . . 204
    XVI. JÜLAI IS ALPHA AND OMEGA . . . 207
    XVII. DIFFERENCES 214
    XVIII. IMMEDIATE JOY [CONVERSION] . . . 217
    XIX. THE IDEAL PREACHER 219
    XX. HONOUR THE WORTHY 223
    XXI. PENTECOST 226
    XXII. BE ONE 229
    XXIII. THE PHYSICIAN 231
    XXIV. WONDERFUL NEWS [TRANSFIGURATION] . . 237
    XXV. KWANYIN — THE UNIVERSAL (HEARER OF
        PRAYER) 239
    XXVI. TOLONI (CALLING DEMONS TO AID BY MAGIC) . 241
    XXVII. KWANYIN'S ROYAL PARENTS . . . 244

CONTENTS

THE NEW TESTAMENT OF HIGHER BUDDHISM

I

GENERAL INTRODUCTION

I. WHY PUBLISH A NEW BOOK ON BUDDHISM?

I HAVE spent forty years in the Far East, during which much time has been devoted to the study of Buddhism in China and Japan.

In publishing this new book on Buddhism, I have no desire to weary students with mere repetition of what has been published before, but have two objects in view.

Firstly, I hope to dispel some of the confusion of thought regarding the relation of Buddhism to Christianity. On this subject the translation of *The Awakening of Faith in the Mahayana School* throws most important light.

For a century past in Europe, it has been well

I

known to students that there were two schools of Buddhism, the Hinayana and the Mahayana.

That Christianity and Buddhism had many truths in common was also well known. Superficial students, however, assumed that because Sakyamuni was born five centuries before Jesus Christ, Christianity had therefore borrowed these truths from Buddhism, not knowing that the Hinayana form of Buddhism was comparatively local and short-lived, while it was the Mahayana school of Buddhism which was so widely adopted in China, Korea, and Japan, lasting to this day. Nor do they know that the Mahayana school, of which Edwin Arnold wrote so beautifully in his *Light of Asia*, was not founded by Sakyamuni five centuries before Christ, but by Ashvagosha at the close of the first century of the Christian era, when communication between East and West was frequent and extensive.

Secondly, I hope to show that in *The Essence of the Lotus Scripture*, as interpreted by Chinese and Japanese "initiated" Buddhists (but not as by the enlarged version in Kern's translation in the *Sacred Books of the East*), we find the same teaching as in the Gospel of St. John in regard to Life, Light, and Love, a teaching which forms a wonderful bridge crossing the chasm between Eastern and Western religion and civilisation.

Max Müller, Bunyiu Nanjio, Takakusu, Edmunds,

and others, in their translations of some of the
leading Mahayana Scriptures, have afforded valuable
material for the study of the extensive common
ground in Buddhism and Christianity. None of
these writings, however, shed greater light than is
given by these two wonderful but hitherto little-
known books in the West, *The Awakening of Faith*,
and *The Essence of the Lotus Scripture*, which have
been for fifteen centuries sources of consolation and
aspiration to countless millions in the Far East.

A translation of *The Awakening of Faith* was
made into English by Zuzuki and published in
1900, but unfortunately without the knowledge of
the Buddhists' true key to the fundamental and
central idea of the book, namely, Chen Jü. This
he translated by the term " Suchness," thus obscur-
ing the meaning of the whole. In my translation,
however, I have followed the meaning given in
a standard Buddhist book, *Wan Fa Kwei Hsin
Luh*, namely, God as The True Model. This
rendering, while faithful to the meaning of the
original, as interpreted by this standard work, at
the same time harmonises most fully with Christian
philosophy and religion.

The Lotus Scripture, in its translation by Kern,
was coloured so much by adaptation to Indian
environment that the essence of its teaching was
obscured. Thus neither of these books has been
fully understood nor appreciated. I do not

translate the whole of the Lotus Scripture, but only that part which is considered by Chinese and Japanese "initiated" Buddhists to be its essence. By following the interpretation of a standard work on *The Awakening of Faith*, and by relying on the judgment of the "initiated" as to the true teaching of the Lotus Scripture, Western readers will be in a better position to understand the vital connection between Christianity and Buddhism, and to pave the way for the one great world-wide religion of the future.

II. Intercommunication in Ancient Times

It is a very common error to think that intercourse between the East and West did not exist until modern times, and that ideas were not transmitted from one to the other. These days of excavations have brought to light proofs of extensive traffic in thought and commerce in early days between distant countries.

In Western Asia, there were great highways, along which great commercial caravans travelled from Babylon to Palestine and Egypt. The discovery of the Tel-el-Amarna correspondence between the Governments of Babylon, Egypt, and the Hittites show there was extensive intercourse between these peoples about B.C. 1400.

There were both overland routes and sea routes

across Europe and Asia about the beginning of the Christian era. The Chinese Chang Kien travelled to the West in the second century B.C. The Commissioners sent by the Emperor Ming Ti in A.D. 61 went to India, passed through many countries, and brought eminent teachers back from India. From Parthia came missionaries to China in the second century A.D.

In our days we have discovered, buried in Turkestan, the Bible of Mani, who once had a very large number of followers in China.

In the eighth century A.D. there was a large trade between Arabia and Canton, and 120,000 Mohammedans, Jews, Christians, and Parsees were massacred in a rebellion there in A.D. 877.

At that time Mohammed's cousin came to China and had an audience with the Emperor, who had in his possession paintings of Christian prophets which he showed to the Arab ambassador.

Dr. Hirth, in his paper in the *Royal Asiatic,* speaks of the considerable trade between China and Socotra and Zanzibar in the eighth century.

We also know of the fleets which sailed from China to Persia and the Red Sea in the days of Marco Polo.

Mr. Mayers, formerly of the British Legation in Peking, has given details of the extensive commerce between China and the west of Asia during the Ming dynasty three centuries ago.

Thus from very early times even distant China (Seres) had intercourse both by land and sea with the West. Buddhist pilgrims, Sung Yun, Iching, and Huen Tsang, travelled westward by land through Central Asia, and some came back by sea, in company with merchant caravans and fleets. Hindu, Parthian, and Nestorian missionaries, to the extent of 2000, lived at Loyang, the capital of China, about a thousand years ago.

Again, as Babylon and India were so near each other, the political, commercial, and religious ideas between them must have been to a large extent common matters of knowledge. Among these the advanced religious teachers of the Jewish prophets in Babylon about the coming Messiah and the kingdom of God must have been fairly well known also.

Before printing was invented, it was impossible to multiply sufficient MS. books for educational purposes. Thus it was that religious teachers adopted the ingenious method of using art as a means of teaching religion. Paintings and sculptures in wood and stone were used to represent their chief gods, leading prophets and saints. Sooner or later, all religions in the East and West, except Islam, adopted this method, and great impetus was given to religious art throughout the world.

Westward, religious education by means of art

is seen in the use of architecture and music. Thus by this intercommunication between distant parts of the earth we find the spread of religious ideas and sacred thought, looking to the Divine as the fountain-head of all hope—ideals common to all mankind—westward as far as the Pacific, and eastward to the Pacific again, completing the whole round of the earth.

III. The Leading of God in Contemporary Religious Movements

The condensation of nebula into the solid earth, the appearance of rocks, of vegetable and animal life, did not take place at different times, but simultaneously all over the earth.

By comparing the dates of great conquerors, of great sages and founders of religions and civilisations, we find that there was a simultaneous movement operating, indicating that they were brought about by causes common to them acting universally. Thousands of years B.C. we find polytheism all over the world, attended by multitudes of religious ceremonies. About the fifth and sixth centuries B.C. there arose in China, in India, in Babylon, in Judea, and in Greece a large number of prophets and sages who laid more emphasis on ethics than on religious ceremonies paid to a multitude of gods. From the beginning of the Christian era onwards for a thousand years, we find monotheism and ethics superseding ancient polytheism and religious ceremonies, in Europe under Christianity, in Western Asia under Mohammedanism, in India producing the Bhagavat Gita, and in the Far East, China, Korea, and Japan, under Confucianism and New Buddhism.

Even the Reformation in Europe is paralleled in China and Japan by a similar antagonism to the then prevailing religions, first against Buddhism and then against Roman Catholicism, when men sought for new light on the problems of human life both in the East and the West.

When the universal empire of Catholicism tried to stamp out the Reformed religion by the most cruel persecutions, God raised up William of Orange, Gustavus Adolphus, and others, to deliver Europe from this oppression.

When military Buddhism and military Catholicism tried to control Japan by political intrigues, God raised up the two great military and civil geniuses Hideyoshi and Ieyasu to deliver their country from tyranny and oppression; while in China they were followed by the all-powerful and all-wise Emperor Kanghi, who saved the Empire from falling into the hands of bigoted religious people, whether of China or of the West.

In our day we are face to face and side by side with the choicest and most enlightened souls, who, while realising the immanence of God, are striving to obtain a glimpse behind the veil into the transcendency of God and recognise the Divine current of spiritual force which inspires all nations and races with modern Life, Light, and Love.

IV. SOME PROMINENT TEACHERS AND TRANSLATORS OF THE MAHAYANA SCHOOL

The most prominent teachers of the Mahayana school are four, namely, Ashvagosha, Nagarguna, Asamgha, and Vasubhandu.

1. Ashvagosha, six centuries after Sakyamuni, about A.D. 100, composed the Mahayana Sraddhotpada Sastra (*The Awakening of Faith*), which is generally regarded as the book which gave rise to the Mahayana school, or New Testament Buddhism.

This was translated into Chinese by Paramartha (A.D. 502–551).

2. Nagarguna, a century after Ashvagosha (about A.D. 160–194), composed the Mahayana Sastra (not translated into Chinese), the Mahapragna Paramita Sastra (Ta Chih Tu Lun or Essays on Wisdom), translated by Kumaragiva in A.D. 402–405, and the Madyamaka Sastra (Chung Lun), also translated by Kumaragiva.

3. Asamgha, three centuries after Ashvagosha, is said to have received from Maitreya, the Buddhist Messiah, the Yogakaria Bhumi Sastra (Yokia Shih

Ti Lun), translated by Huen Tsang in 646–647. He himself composed the Mahayana Samparig Raha Sastra (Nie Ta Ching Lun), translated by Paramartha in A.D. 563.

4. Vasubhandu, the younger brother of Asamgha, composed—

    (*a*) The Anitagus Sutro Padesa, translated by Bodhiruki in 529. (Vasubhandu, on account of this book, is regarded as the second patriarch of the Amitabha school, Nagarguna being the first.)

    (*b*) The Buddha Gotra Sastra (Fo Shing Lun), translated by Paramartha.

    (*c*) The Sadharma Pundarika Sutra Sastra (a commentary on the Lotus Scripture).

    (*d*) The Nirvana Sastra (Ta Pan Nie King Lun), translated by Dharmabodhi in the Eastern Wu dynasty 386–550.

    (*e*) Vagrakkhedika Sutra Sastra (the Diamond Classic commentary), translated by Bodheruki in 509.

    (*f*) Dasabhumika Sastra (Shih Ti King Lun), translated by Bodheruki.

    (*g*) Vidyamatra Siddhi Tri Dasa Sastra (thirty verses), translated by Huen Tsang in 648, on which ten teachers compiled a commentary.

The works of Vasubhandu are said to number one thousand in all.

There is no need to give a list of translators of Buddhist Scriptures from Sanscrit into Chinese, as they are given in Bunyiu Nanjio's Catalogue of the Buddhist Tripitaka, Appendix II. But I will mention one, as of special interest, as a small link in the historical connection between Christianity and New or Higher Buddhism. It is Anshikao, a Parthian prince who gave up his kingdom in order to become a missionary in China A.D. 148.

He translated from ninety-five to one hundred and seventy-six works into Chinese, of which the names of fifty-five are given in Bunyiu Nanjio's catalogue. Anshikao's aunt was a hostage in Rome during the time that Callistus was Pope. Among the books translated by Anshikao is one on the Buddhist Messiah (Mi Le Fo), and Pope Callistus seemed inclined to believe that its teaching was, in the main, the same as that which was current among the Christians of the West at that early date (see Professor Lloyd's *Wheat among Tares*, chap. xi.).

The fact that the Pope in Rome was familiar with Buddhist teaching is another proof that transfer of religious ideas from the Far West to the Far East was quite possible in those early days.

As to the others, they, like all translators, could not eliminate the personal element of their age and environment. It is only as we can penetrate beyond this that we can discern the true meaning of these ancient writings.

V. Buddhist Trinities

In Judaism, we see one wondrous development of Monotheism into a Trinity in Unity of Christianity which is the chief religious force in the world to-day. In Buddism we see two wondrous developments—first, Atheism into Theism; and secondly, the development of that Theism into a Monotheistic Trinity in Unity. In the last chapter of the Epilogue of the Lotus Gospel the constant reference is to the "great," or advanced, or new religion as the only hope of salvation for the world, in contrast to the "small," or elementary, or old religion originally founded by Sakyamuni. This great religion is so marvellously like Christianity in its central teaching that it might well be called Pre-Nestorian Christianity.

Buddhism possesses two groups of Trinities, which it is most important to distinguish, as the fundamental idea of the one is salvation by man's own strength, while that of the other is salvation by superhuman help.

The first group, mainly of the Hinayana school, is the Sakyamuni Trinity—

Sakyamuni in the centre,

Puhien Pusa on his right hand, riding on an elephant,

Wen Shu Pusa on his left hand, riding on a lion.

Originally, Sakyamuni was the Hindu prince

who left his palace and throne in order to discover salvation from the sea of trouble and sorrow in transmigration. This salvation he declared was by means of man's own effort without any help from above.

The original teaching taught by him and held by the Hinayana school, however, was, according to Buddhist historians, of comparatively short duration. About the beginning of the Christian era, Sakyamuni was worshipped as God, and consequently the character of Buddhism was from that time completely changed.

Puhien is regarded as the embodiment of goodwill. Wen Shu as the embodiment of wisdom.

The second group, mainly of the Mahayana school, is the Amitabha Trinity—

> Amitabha in the centre,
> Ta Shih Chih on his right hand,
> Kwanyin on his left.

In the Book of Revelation, heaven is described as a place which is holy, where there is nothing impure, and where there is no need of the sun and moon, for God is the light of it. God is described as the One that liveth for ever and ever, the Alpha and Omega.

Turning to the New Buddhist Scriptures, we find heaven is called the Happy Land, the Beautiful Land, the Pure Land where Amitabha (Omito Fu) reigns. He is described as one of Boundless Light and Boundless Age, without birth or death, without beginning or end—the Everlasting.

The Book of Revelation and the New Testament describe Jesus Christ as having the keys of death, who opens and no man can shut, who shuts and no man can open; who was, is, and is to come; who has received all power in heaven and earth, and who sits on the right hand of God.

Turning to the Scriptures of New, or Higher, Buddhism, they describe the Chinese Ta Shih Chih, Japanese Dai Seishi, as follows :—

God has two supreme heavenly beings as counsellors. The name of One is Kwanyin, and the name of the Other is Ta Shih Chih (the Great Mighty One), who always sit on each side of Him. God took counsel with them about past, present, and future affairs of the universe, and desired that they should separate from Him and go and become incarnate (fên shin, which is the very expression many missionaries use in describing the Three Persons of the Trinity) in one of the worlds and help Him to save it, without losing their original unity and state (*The Great Amitabha Scripture*, Nanjio's Catalogue, No. 203, chap. xxxvi.). (Cf. John xvi. 28.)

The Scripture of Boundless Age (Cat. No. 133) says of Ta Shih Chih that he can put an end to the Karma chain of endless births and deaths caused by sin, by removing sin altogether, without

needing a single re-birth, but go straight to the Pure
Land of Paradise, and live for ever there (Meditation 12).   In one instance I have seen an image of
Mileh Fo (the Buddhist Messiah) taking the place of
Ta Shih Chih opposite to Kwanyin, as if the two were
one and the same.   But the identification of these
two with the Great Physician requires more study.

Again, St. Paul in Romans, after describing the
whole creation groaning and travailing, writes : " The
Holy Spirit helps our infirmity and makes inter-
cession for us with groanings that cannot be uttered,"
and " If God be for us, who can be against us ? "

Turning to the Scriptures of the New Buddhism,
we find they say that from time to time in all
classes of society, from the highest to the lowest,
there are men and women who are moved with
pity towards their fellow-men, and are inspired
to devote all their energies for the salvation of
others.   This Inspirer of their highest and holiest
thoughts they call Kwanyin in China and Kwannon
in Japan, which means the One who looks down
upon human suffering and is the Inspirer of men
and women to save their fellows.   Sometimes this
Inspirer is represented by a male Manjusri, and
sometimes by a female, the goddess of Mercy.   But
the true meaning is the Divine Inspirer of both
men and women.

Thus we find in these three a complete identification of the attributes of the Christian Trinity

in the New Buddhism (see below, Section 6, Kwanyin, for fuller account).

In the West, God is generally spoken of as masculine—the Father God.

In India, the gods are both masculine and feminine.

In the Far East, the love of God is described most fully in the feminine character, the goddess of Mercy.

The famous Buddhist Triad of—

Buddha (the absolute, supreme God),

The Law (eternal in the universe),

The Priesthood (to teach and practise the Law), is of a different category altogether, and, comprehensive in its classification, belongs to all religions.

VI. KWANYIN, THE SO-CALLED GODDESS OF MERCY, OR A FAR EASTERN VERSION OF THE HOLY SPIRIT

As the fullest story of Kwanyin is to be found in the 25th chapter of the Lotus Scripture, and as Kwanyin figures so largely among the Buddhist deities, I give a translation from the original Chinese of the whole of that chapter, as it is most important to explain who Kwanyin is. It is as follows :—

Once the Saint Wuchini Shekayamati (exhaustless meaning) rose from his seat, removed his robe from his right shoulder, folded his palms, looked towards God, and said: "World-honoured One, why is Kwanyin called the Hearer of the world's prayers?" God answered him: "Good man, if innumerable beings are suffering all kinds of troubles, and with all their heart call on Kwanyin, Kwanyin immediately listens and delivers them. Whoever lays hold of this Name, even if they enter a great fire it will not burn them. This is because Kwanyin is a Divine power.

"If floating on a great flood and call on this Name, they will reach a shallow place.

"If many merchants seeking gold and silver, white stones of adularia, agate, coral, amber, pearls, and such-like treasures, and when sailing on the ocean meet a typhoon blowing their ships adrift among cannibal tribes, if there is even a single one in the ship who calls on the Name of Kwanyin, all those on board will be delivered from danger. For this reason Kwanyin is called the 'Hearer of the world's prayers.'

"If a man should be about to suffer hurt from any one and calls on Kwanyin, the weapons used to harm, whether sword or spear, will at once break in pieces and the threatened sufferer be saved.

"If a world full of demons are about to attack men, when they hear any calling on the Name of Kwanyin, these demons cannot then look at them with evil intent, much less harm them.

2

" Again, if one has or has not committed a crime, is handcuffed in stocks, examined and bound, and calls on the Name of Kwanyin, the bands will be broken, and he delivered.

" If in a world full of cruel robbers, and the leader of a caravan provides necessary and many treasures for the journey, and goes through dangerous roads, and there is one man who sings this hymn to Kwanyin, none of the good men need have any fear; they should with all their heart call upon the Name of Kwanyin, and Kwanyin will be able to make all of them fearless. If they thus call on this Name, then they will be delivered from the cruel robbers. The robbers, on hearing the merchants all saying, ' I believe in Kwanyin, the Hearer of the world's prayers,' leave, and the merchants are at once delivered.

" Wuchini, I tell you Kwanyin's Divine power is great and sublime [cf. Ps. cvii.].

" If men are led too much by their passions, by constant thought of and the worship of Kwanyin these lusts can be suppressed.

" If men are too hot-tempered, by constant thought of and the worship of Kwanyin they get rid of anger.

"If men are stupid and foolish, by constant thought of and the worship of Kwanyin they will get rid of their foolishness. I tell you, Wuchini, Kwanyin has this great Divine power and majesty in abundance, therefore all men should think of Kwanyin.

" If a woman desires a son and worships Kwanyin, she will get a happy, virtuous, and wise son. If she desires a daughter, she will get a good and beautiful daughter, who will be rooted in virtue, loved and respected by all. I tell you, Wuchini, Kwanyin has this power. If all men respect and worship Kwanyin, their happiness will not fail them, therefore all men should hallow the Name. I tell you, Wuchini, if a man hallows saints to the number of 620,000, or as numerous as the sands of the Ganges, and then worships each with food and clothing, lodgings and medicine, what do you think of the merit of such a man or woman ? Is it not great ? "

Wuchini answered, " Yes, Lord, it is very great."

God said: "Yet if a man hallows Kwanyin's Name but once, and worships Kwanyin, the blessing of the two are equal and cannot end for millions of years. Wuchini, I tell you that the hallowing of Kwanyin's Name will receive the benefit of infinite blessings."

Saint Wuchini said: " World-honoured One, tell me—why does Kwanyin preach the Law ? Why is all this power of goodness ? "

God answered: " My good man, if there are men in any nation who shall be saved by Divine incarnation or indwelling, Kwanyin becomes manifest as Divine, and inspires them with the Law.

" If it is necessary that doctors of theology should be saved, Kwanyin appears as a doctor of theology and preaches the Law to them.

" If it is necessary that Buddhists of the old school should be saved, Kwanyin appears as a Buddhist of the old school and preaches the Law to them.

" If it is necessary that a Brahman be saved, Kwanyin appears as a Brahman to preach the Law to him.

" If it is necessary that Indra is to be saved, then Kwanyin appears as Indra and preaches the Law to him.

" If it is necessary to save free disembodied spirits, Kwanyin appears as a free disembodied spirit and preaches the Law to them.

" If it is necessary to save the great generals of heaven, Kwanyin appears as a great general of heaven and preaches the Law to them.

" If it is necessary to save gods of luck, Kwanyin appears as a god of luck and preaches the Law to them.

" If it is necessary to save small kings, Kwanyin appears as a small king and preaches the Law to them.

" If it is necessary to save leaders, Kwanyin appears as a leader and preaches the Law to them.

" If it is necessary to save private scholars, Kwanyin appears as a private scholar and preaches the Law to them.

" If it is necessary to save officials, Kwanyin appears as an official and preaches the Law to them.

" If it is necessary to save Brahmins, Kwanyin appears as a Brahmin and preaches the Law to them.

" If it is necessary to save priests or nuns or novices, Kwanyin appears as a priest or nun or a novice and preaches the Law to them.

" If it is necessary to save the wives of leaders, scholars, officials, Brahmins, Kwanyin appears as a woman and preaches the Law to them.

" If it is necessary to save young men or young women, Kwanyin appears as a young man or a young woman and preaches the Law to them.

" If it is necessary to save devas, dragons, night-goblins, kandapos, asuras, kialoulos, kinaloulos, kinnalos, moholokias, men and not-men, Kwanyin appears like them and preaches the Law to them.

" If it is necessary to save angels who hold sceptres, Kwanyin appears as one holding a sceptre and preaches the Law to them.

" Thus, Wuchini, Kwanyin accomplishes merit in all sorts of forms, appearing in all lands to save all. On this account all of you should with one mind worship Kwanyin, the Hearer of the world's prayers, the great prayer-answering God.

" When in fear and great difficulties, Kwanyin can make you fearless, therefore all in this evil world call Kwanyin 'the Giver of courage, the Fearless One'" [cf. Matt. x. 19, 20].

Wuchini spoke to God and said: "World-honoured One, now I must worship Kwanyin." He took off from his neck the precious pearls and ornaments which had cost a hundred thousand ounces of gold, and offered them to Kwanyin, saying, "Benevolent One, receive this gift of a necklace of precious pearls." But Kwanyin was unwilling to receive it. Wuchini again said: "Benevolent One, for our sakes please receive this necklace"; and God also said to Kwanyin: "For the sake of Wuchini and the four classes, devas, dragons, yehtsas, kandapos, together with asuras, kialoulos, kinalos, moholokias, men and not-men, receive this necklace."

Then Kwanyin for the sake of all these received the necklace and divided it into two. One-half she gave to Sakyamuni and one-half she gave to the temple of the God of all Grace. Wuchini Kwanyin has this Divine power of choice in herself, *voluntarily* to come to save this evil world.

Then Wuchini composed a hymn of one hundred lines of ten words each in her honour.

After this, Saint Wuchini arose, went towards God, and said: "World-honoured One, whoever makes known to all beings the character of Kwanyin, the Hearer of the world's prayers, Kwanyin's voluntary service and Kwanyin's miraculous power universally manifested, his merit will be great." God answered : " This time of the universal influence of Kwanyin will enable all living beings to obtain the supremely correct wisdom of the soul."

VII. Two very Striking Sets of Vows

Both the Christians and the Buddhists regard their chief object of worship as Divine and full of compassion for human suffering. The Christians speak of their Saviour as voluntarily leaving the glory of heaven, where He was equal with God, and coming down, lower than an angel, to be man, suffering the shameful death of the cross for those who were so cruel as to crucify Him, and praying for them : " Father, forgive them ; for they know not what they do " (Phil. ii., Luke xxiii.).

The Apostle Paul so pitied his fellow-men that he wished himself " accursed from Christ " for his brethren (Rom. ix. 3).

Again, when our Lord was about to leave this world, He said : " Let not your heart be troubled . . . I go to prepare a place for you . . . that where I am, there ye may be also " (John xiv. 1–3).

When devout Buddhists read these sentiments, they find much that commends itself to them as of exceptionally high merit.

On the other hand, when the Christian reads the vows of Amitabha (Dharmakara), which are here summarised as saying he did not wish to go to heaven if his followers could not enjoy the same forty-six perfections as he had, namely, all power, all wisdom, roaming through innumerable worlds in boundless space of glory with happiness unspeakable, with all wishes gratified, with boundless life, light, peace, and joy; where life is without faintness and without end, without sin, without pain, without grief, without ignorance, etc. (*Sacred Books of the East*, vol. xlix. part ii. 12).

Or when they read the twelve vows of the Buddhist Great Physician, which are here summarised from a Chinese Buddhist standard work hitherto untranslated into English, namely :—

1. To descend to earth to make men godlike.
2. To enlighten the ignorant.
3. To supply all human wants.
4. To teach the New and Living Way.
5. To save men from hell and make them holy.
6. To heal men from all diseases.
7. To befriend the friendless.
8. To give hope to womankind.
9. To lead back the erring in thought.
10. To deliver the erring in action.
11. To feed the hungry and thirsty.
12. To feed hungry Spirits with spiritual food, and clothe them with garments of righteousness.

Yo Shih Liu Li Kwang Julai King, which has also the names of his twelve Generals (Apostles ?).

When devout Christians read these sentiments, they will find much that will commend itself to them as of exceptional merit, and will remind them strongly of the teaching of their own Great Physician.

Thus both Christians and Buddhists, by dwelling on their respective ideals rather than on their respective imperfections, will find themselves inspired to co-operate and exert themselves more than ever before for the salvation of their fellowmen, and to study each other's most sacred books. There are dry bones in both religions. What is needed is the Creative Spirit of the Christians, called the Merciful Kwanyin by the Buddhists, to make these dry bones live again!

VIII. The Deification of Sakyamuni the Atheist !

When Buddha began to teach he appeared exactly as teachers, professors, or leaders of thought appear in our day. He had a theory of life which commended itself to a large class of disciples, who in turn commended the same theory to their disciples, just like Darwin, Herbert Spencer, or Mrs. Eddy.

The theory was—

1. That the suffering of the world should be removed.

2. That the suffering could only be removed by removing the cause.

3. That the cause was, desire of anything but rest of soul.

4. That this rest of soul was only in thought ecstasy. This view resulted, after its adoption by Asoka, in a rapid widespread system of philanthropy throughout his empire. But Buddhist historians say that this theory of life after experience of two or three centuries lost its charm over the minds of men, till a new doctrine was added to the scheme of life, namely—

1. Help from God to save oneself and others from suffering.

2. Communion with God, which gave the highest ecstatic rest to the soul.

3. Partaking of the nature of God by new birth, so as to become Divine and Immortal oneself.

This was called the Mahayana school of Buddhism containing the Amitabha or Pure Land Doctrine. But the old Buddhists belonging to the Hinayana school were unwilling that their Teacher should occupy a second place, therefore they deified Sakyamuni and worshipped him exactly as the Mahayana school worshipped God, as we see in the Lotus Scripture. While they say Sakyamuni, they mean God throughout. From that time of the transfiguration of Buddha, Buddhism took a new lease of life and commended itself to the heart of most of the millions of Asia. Thus we see that its theology is Christian in everything almost but its nomenclature. Ashvagosha was the Apostle Paul of Buddhism, and lived only about fifty years after Paul. Where Ashvagosha got his ideas we do not know. Some say from the Apostle Thomas, who is supposed to have been together with him in the court of Gondophorus or Kanishka. But we await further light on the historic meeting-place of Christianity and New Buddhism before more definite pronouncement can be made. Still, the amazing fact remains that the deification of Sakyamuni the atheist took place at this time, and the Old original Buddhism from this time on was superseded by the New, which believed in God.

IX. The Influence of Buddhism

It is both beneficial and hurtful. These influences are now made clear by the winnowing fan of comparative religion.

1. *Beneficial*

(1) It made men think of eternal things as vastly more important than temporary perishing things.

(2) It made men feel that their eternal happiness or misery depended mainly on character (Karma regulating re-births). The result was a universal scheme of philanthropy to both men and beasts under Asoka.

(3) It promised answers to prayers, anticipating modern Christian science by firm belief in Amitabha, in Yo Shih Fu (the Great Physician), and in Kwanyin.

(4) It makes men tender-hearted and think how they can save men from sin and suffering.

(5) It made men go forth as missionaries to save mankind—west to Egypt and Europe, in Gnosticism south to Ceylon and Java, north to Central Asia and Mongolia, and east to China, Korea, and Japan.

(6) It adopted the most superb *kindergarten* system of teaching to be found in all the world. Grecian art from Gandara was developed in India and at Borobudur in Java. Then it was developed in China and Japan, till we find nothing superior to it for religious teaching anywhere in the world.

2. *Hurtful*

(1) Buddhism made a gigantic blunder when it impugned the wisdom of God in creating sex, which is not only human but animal and vegetable, holding that the exercise of natural functions for reproduction to be sinful, instead of being talents to be rightly used. The celebrated Chinese philosopher Chu Hi, a thousand years ago rightly pointed out that if all became Buddhists there would be an end of the human race, after one generation had passed away.

(2) The corollaries of this theory—asceticism, monasticism, and fasting—have been tried on a world-wide scale, and have lasted for thousands of years to a large extent in Christian as well as in Buddhist countries, and are all serious mistakes, breaking instead of observing the eternal laws of nature.

(3) Buddhist theory of this world and of the universe as described elaborately in its literature (see Guide to Buddhahood, Devalokas, etc., translated into English by the present Author) is not justified by modern research, but, on the contrary, is contradicted. Not even Buddhist intelligent men believe in them now, as not any of them can be claimed as discoveries. They are only childish dreams, pure castles in the air.

(4) Buddhist theories of Gnostic hierarchies of countless superhuman beings in the different parts of the universe are only speculations of men with lively imaginations without any facts to support them, even after thousands of years of experiment. The exercise of millions of minds on a barren speculation is an incalculable loss to the progress of the human race.

3. *The Winnowing Fan of Comparative Religion and Experience*

(1) The doctrine of Karma, to be worked by man alone, as taught in the ancient Hinayana school of

Buddhism, when it met with a new religion which taught that the Divine factor was greater than mere human Karma, admitted its truth, and from that time was dated the Mahayana doctrine of united action of human Karma and Divine Grace, which have captured the best intellects of the Far East until they became obscured by a reaction of ancient undeveloped Buddhism, again leaving the soul still to grope its way in a thick fog.

(2) Asceticism, monasticism, and fasting are now giving way to marriage of priests and nuns and the establishment of colleges where men and women are taught on equal footing instead of the Buddhist idea of the inferiority of women.

(3) Ancient religious problems giving way to more profitable modern problems of capital and labour, socialism and internationalism, ideal education and righteousness with God and man, firmly fixed in human hearts as the foundation of the kingdom of God on earth.

4. *Its Influence on Taoism*

The superior influence of the Lotus Gospel over all the other Buddhist Scriptures is not only seen in the fact that apparently all the Buddhist temples give it a place of honour in Japan, but even the Taoists in China have been so impressed with its value that, though they did not reprint it, they have written another after its model which they call the Taoist Lotus Gospel.

Its authorship is attributed to Lü Tsu, who spiritualised the Taoist religion after the manner of Nestorian teaching which flourished in the capital of China (Sianfu) in his days, and was the founder of so many semi-Christian secret sects that worship a white-faced God (till forbidden to be white by the present dynasty), who answers prayer and heals all diseases much like the Christ of Christian scientists.

If we ask wherein the extraordinary influence of the Lotus Gospel consists, I would say—though it speaks of many mansions in heaven, with bodies twenty-five miles high, living one thousand years, and other apparent extravagances, still its main value seems to be in confirming—

1. Men's faith in its Divine power to deliver men from the chains of endless transmigration and be able to go to paradise at once.

2. Men's faith in its power to give everlasting life.

3. Men's faith in its healing power equal to all that Christian scientists claim.

4. Men's faith in its magic power to insure persons against all accidents and dangers to body and soul.

5. Men's faith in its power to unite men with God and share in His miraculous power over all things.

6. Men's faith in its power to overcome all evil spirits and devils.

7. Men's faith in the equality of all men before God, in hearing the prayers of rich and poor alike.

Both the Buddhist and Taoist versions quote the same sign as evidence of its being from God, namely, "Above comes forth water, and below comes forth fire." Again, "Above there comes forth fire and below water" (*Lotus Gospel*, chap. xxvii.).

The meaning here is not apparent. But it reminds one of the two miraculous symbols of the Holy Spirit—the water of life which flows from the sanctuary of God for the healing of the nations (Ezek. xlvii. and John vii. 37–39). And again one of the seraphims having a live coal from the altar touched Isaiah's lips, and said, "Lo, this hath touched thy lips; and thine iniquity is taken away." And again, cloven tongues as of fire filled the disciples with the Holy Ghost and with marvellous enthusiasm for the salvation of all men (Acts ii. 2–4). Thus as fire and water produce steam, the chief factor in modern industries, so does burning gratitude to God and desire to benefit our fellow-men produce intense enthusiasm, the chief factor in the spiritual progress of man. New Buddhism in the Far East as well as Christianity in the Far West claims a large share of this Divine enthusiasm for the good of the human race.

X. The Religion of the Future

We Christians believe that the kingdoms of this world shall become the kingdom of our Lord, and that then there will be but One Faith.   Meanwhile, we look out on the religious world as it exists to-day, and note that among all the habits of men none are more permanent than the religious.   It is the habit of caste in India carried on for millenniums that makes it second nature to the Hindu, as if caste were as fixed as the stars in the heavens or as immovable as the earth beneath them.

The   same   is   true   of   Chinese   religions — Confucianism,   Buddhism,   and   Taoism;   and   is equally   true   of   Christianity,   Islam,   and   the   minor Reformed   branches   of   Sikhs   and   Bahaists.   The children   of   all   lands   follow   their   parents   from age   to   age,   not   so   much   from   knowledge   as   from habit.

The Buddhists believe that Sakyamuni was all-wise, therefore   taught   the   highest   truths   for mankind.

Confucianists vaguely believe that the Emperor of China is the only son of Heaven, and therefore all nations should obey him.

The Shintoists believe that the Emperor of Japan is different in kind from ordinary mortals —a descendant of the gods, therefore superior to all sovereigns of earth.

3

The Pope believes that he represents God on earth, and that all rulers should obey him.

The Mohammedans believe that Mohammed is the last prophet of God to men, and that all men should obey him.

The Sikhs and the Bahaists believe the same of the founders of their religions.

It is only once in five hundred or a thousand years that a man arrives with strength enough to change the religious custom of many generations as a result of study and knowledge of the need of the times. So long as national intercourse was partial, these religious founders stereotyped the habit of their respective religions in local districts or nations, until now we have about seven men in all the world who claim obedience from all the rest.

The time of universal intercourse dawned upon mankind with the advent of steam and electricity within the last century. With this there has arisen the feeling that the next step in religious evolution is not a monopoly of any one of these competitive religions but a federation of all, on a basis that acknowledges with gratitude all that is best in the past in different parts of the earth as Divine, and then finally following the one which surpasses all the rest in authority and in usefulness to the human race.

There would be no difficulty in getting the most

intelligent to recognise Moses and the prophets of Israel, Confucius and Mencius, the Sages of China, Mohammed, God's ambassador to the Arabs, as all sent of God. And the final step in religion is foreshadowed by the firm belief of Hindus, Buddhists, and Christians, that the supreme Saviour of men must be God Incarnate. Latently, if not expressed, Confucianism, Taoism, and Shintoism base their claim to obedience on the belief that their teaching is derived from Heaven, where alone Power, Wisdom, Justice, and Mercy are to be found in perfection.

The Religion of the future which will satisfy all nations and all races will not be born of any party cry, but will be born from the habit of looking at the highest and permanent elements in all religions and gladly recognising all that helps to save man, body, soul, and spirit, individually or collectively, as Divine.

The whole intelligent world is getting tired of the struggle concerning the different doctrines and practices of the various religions and their sub-divisions into many hundreds of sects, but all are eager to know what light any or all of them can throw on—

How to deliver one-tenth of the world from poverty and oppression.

How to deliver one-half of the world from violent men, who produce strikes, riots, rebellions, and wars.

How to deliver more than half of the world from

ignorance and superstition, so that the fruits of the best knowledge God has given us may be reaped.

How to deliver all human hearts from the disease of selfishness and sin, that they may be made right with God and man.

To answer these questions aright is to begin the establishment of the kingdom of God on earth, which Jesus Christ commanded His disciples to preach, and this is the one Great Religion of the future.

XI. RELIGIOUS ART

Under the influence of the Mosaic command forbidding images, Christian art did not develop early in the West.   But in the Far East, where there was no such commandment, there arose a marvellous development which can be traced from Greece to Gandara, India, China, and Japan.

Any one wishing to study high - class early Christian art searches in vain for it in the churches of Christendom before A.D. 500, but if one desires to see the great visions of the Book of Revelation illustrated worthily in art, one should visit the Buddhist temples around Nara and Kioto, where art flourished as a most powerful handmaid to religion before printing had been invented and before education had become general.

II

THE AWAKENING OF FAITH

TRANSLATOR'S INTRODUCTION

I. One of the Great Books of the World, Ta Ching Ki Shin Lun

This is the title of one of the most important books in the world. A Japanese scholar has translated it *The Awakening of Faith*. It might also be rendered *The Mahayana Faith*, or *The Faith of the New Buddhism*. Its importance is apparent when we consider the fact that of the 26,000 Buddhist monks and nuns in Japan no less than 17,000 of them belong to the Pure Land School and the True School, which regard this book as their fountain and origin.

Its importance is still more apparent when we consider that its doctrines are the fundamental ones of the Mahayana Faith, which is by far the chief school of Buddhism, not only in Japan, but also in China, where are the great majority of the

Buddhists of the world. If we estimate the value of books by the number of adherents to their doctrines, then, after the Bible, the Koran, the Confucian Classics, and the Vedas, this volume, about the size of the Gospel of Mark, ranks next, or fifth, among the sacred books of the world.

The great value of the book is also apparent when we remember that the Eastern World had been driven to general despair by the atheistic doctrines of primitive Buddhism called the Hinayana school, and that it was by the doctrines of this book, which gave rise to the Mahayana school of New Buddhism, that a gospel of great hope was preached to the greater part of the Eastern Asiatic continent.   Its new doctrines were that of the One Soul immanent for good in all the universe, that of a Divine Helper of men, of individual immortality and growth in the likeness of God, of the importance of faith in God to produce good works, and that of the willingness of the best spirits to make sacrifices to save others—the very subjects which in these modern days still occupy the attention of the most thoughtful men of the world.

The book is Brahministic and Buddhistic, Indian and Western in some aspects of philosophic thought. It is profoundly philosophic, reminding one strongly of Hegel, Berkeley, and G. Gore in the earlier part, and is harder to understand than Bishop Butler's famous *Analogy*; yet very practical in the latter part, therefore it has great importance arising from its high and extensive range of view.

If it be, as it is more and more believed, that the Mahayana Faith is not Buddhism, properly so-called, but an Asiatic form of the same gospel of our Lord and Saviour Jesus Christ, in Buddhistic nomenclature, differing from the Old Buddhism just as the New Testament differs from the Old, then it commands a world-wide interest, for in it we find an adaptation of Christianity to ancient thought in Asia, and the deepest bond of union between the different races of the East and the West, namely, the bond of a common religion.   Both Christianity and the New Buddhism hold to the transcendent and the immanent forms of God; but the East emphasises more of the immanent form, while the West emphasises more of the transcendent.   The almost universal reception of the doctrines contained in this book by both the East and the West con-stitutes to my mind its highest claim to our attention; for thereby we are brought face to face with a solution of the stupendous practical problem of uniting all races in one bond of religious charity !

II. THE EVOLUTION AND DEVOLUTION OF BUDDHISM

The evolution of Buddhism is seen in the New Buddhism superseding the Old, and the devolution in the attempt by later writers to combine the Primitive with the Advanced, an absurd anachronism and impossibility. This will be apparent from the study of the different schools of Buddhism.

The most common division of Buddhism is that into the smaller (Hinayana), or Primitive Buddhism, and the greater (Mahayana) or Advanced Buddhism.

During Gautama Buddha's life there were no books of his teaching written, but according to a Japanese book on Buddhism called *Pa-chung-kangyao*, published in A.D. 1319, tradition says that during the first four hundred years after Gautama Buddha's death (B.C. 543), the Hinayana school flourished greatly, while the Mahayana was not known. But five hundred years after Buddha's death, Maming (Ashvagosha) wrote the book on *The Mahayana Faith*. The Mahayana school then began to flourish everywhere, while the Hinayana went under a cloud. This makes the rise of the Mahayana school contemporaneous with the rise of Christianity.

Besides this broad division into the Hinayana and the Mahayana schools, there are other divisions of Buddhism which are interesting to know, as they indicate the development and growth of religious ideas in the Buddhist religion, just as in the Christian and in every other religion, and also their decay when Buddhist learning was neglected. For example, in China the Tientai school of

Buddhism, with its headquarters in the mountains / of Chêkiang province, divides Buddhism into four schools, namely—

1. The *Tsang Chiao*, Primitive Buddhism (*i.e.* the Hinayana).

2. *Tung Chiao*, Buddhism in a transition state.

3. *Piêh Chiao*, New Buddhism (*i.e.* the Mahayana).

4. *Yuan Chiao*, the complete religion of all the schools.

The Hsien Shou school of Buddhism—founded by followers of Fa Tsang, called also Hsien Shou, the third patriarch after Wên Shu Pusa, the great Buddhist saint of Wutai, in Shansi, who died A.D. 627 and is specially worshipped by the Mongols—divides Buddhism into five schools, namely—

1. The *Siao Chiao*, or Primitive Buddhism (the Hinayana).

2. *Shih Chiao*, or the Beginning of True Religion (transition state).

3. The *Chung Chiao*, or the Final Development of the True Religion (the Mahayana).

4. The *Tun Chiao*, or the School of Meditation, founded by the last Buddhist patriarch Ta Mo, A.D. 529, is not mentioned separately in the Tientai classification.

5. The *Yuan Chiao*, or the Complete Religion of all the schools.

Generally speaking, the classifications of both agree. But the Tientai school in the province of Chêkiang regards the *Lien-hua-king* or the *Lotus Classic* as their chief scripture, while the Hsien Shou school on the north regards the *Hua-yen-king* as their chief scripture. But both these chief scriptures are said to have their origin in the *Ki Shin Lun*, the book which we now translate under the name of the *New Buddhist Faith*, called in Sanskrit the *Mahayana sraddhotpada shastra*. These classifications are rather ancient. There is a great dearth of books on the subject of modern schools of Buddhism showing the decline of Buddhism in China during the last two dynasties, but there are writers now at work to give the later history of Buddhism in China and to bring it down to date.

In Japan, while Buddhism is divided into the two great schools—the *True School*, by which one seeks salvation by reliance on self, and the *Pure Land School*, by which one seeks salvation by the help of God—all Buddhists are now subdivided into twelve sects. An outline of each of these was given by one of the leading men in each school, and Bunyiu Nanjio, M.A. (Oxon), the ablest Sanskrit scholar then in Japan, translated them into English and published them in 1886 under the name of *A Short History of the Twelve Japanese Buddhist Sects*.

Most of these sects, like the Romanists, forbid
their priests to marry; but others, like the Pro-
testants, give their priests perfect liberty to marry
or not as they please.   Some sects expect to work
out their own salvation with fear and trembling,
saying that whatsoever a man sows that shall he
also reap—the Karma of the Old Buddhism—while
other sects say that repentance and faith in God
can far outstrip all independent efforts at salvation.
Some of the sects insist on incessant study, and, like
the Positivists, expect their followers to be en-
cyclopædias of all knowledge; while others again
are only expected to repeat O-mi-to-Fo, like ourselves in our Western religions, who think the
" Hail Mary " or " Only Believe " sufficient doctrines
equally absurd or profound according to our stand-
point of observing them or of using them.   Thus
we see a striking parallelism in the development of
religion in the West and in the East—signs of life
as well as of decay.

III. How I came to Translate this Book

The story is of no small interest.   In 1884 I
visited Nanking in company with my revered
friend, David Hill, to see the Viceroy, and
to persuade him to interest himself in securing
religious freedom for Christians and immunity
from persecution.   Whilst there, I sought for

some Buddhist books which I could not procure in the north of China. I learnt that a Buddhist Book Society had been started in Nanking, Soochow, and Hangchow, three of the leading cities in Central China, in order to replace those destroyed during the Tai Ping Rebellion. Of the three societies, the most important was that at Nanking, and the prime mover of the whole three societies lived there. His name was Yang Wên Hui. I called on him, and found him the most intelligent Buddhist I had ever met. He had been several years in Europe as treasurer to the Chinese Embassy when Marquis Tseng represented China in England and France. Mr. Yang had had interviews with Max Müller and Julien and Bunyiu Nanjio of Tokio, who had studied under Max Müller. Thus, besides being well acquainted with the Buddhist authorities in China, he was personally acquainted with the best authorities in Europe and Japan. Mr. Yang was not a Buddhist priest, but a Confucianist with the B.A. (siutsai) degree, and was only a lay Buddhist.

I said to him, "How is it that you, with a Confucian degree, should have ever become a Buddhist?" His answer was striking: "I am surprised that you, a missionary, should ask me that question, for you must know that Confucianism shirks some of the most important questions. It only deals with human affairs now, not with the superhuman." "But do you mean to say that

Buddhism answers those questions?" He said,
"Yes." "Where?" I asked again. He answered,
"In a book called *The Awakening of Faith*. That
book converted me from Confucianism to Buddhism."
"Have you that book for sale here?" I asked.
"Yes," he replied, and brought the book and laid
it in my hands. Finding him to be most thoroughly
conversant with the relative value of the various
Buddhist books, I asked him to select for me some
dozen works which he considered most important.
Having paid for them, I returned to my inn.
Shortly after, the box containing all my purchases
arrived. I looked for the book on *The Awakening
of Faith*, and began reading it, and sat up reading
it till the small hours of the morning. I cried to
my friend Hill, who was also sitting up late at
work, "This is a Christian book and most interesting." "Christian?" my friend cried, with great
doubt. "You are reading your own thoughts into
the book!" "Well, then," I said, "how do you explain these passages?" pointing to some to which
there was no ready explanation.

Three months later I was in a bookseller's shop
in Edinburgh, and, looking through his new books,
I came across Beal's little book on Buddhism, then
just published. Turning up a certain chapter in it,
I found that he referred to *The Awakening of Faith*
as a pseudo-Christian book which it was desirable
to have translated!

Years passed by. In 1891 I was transferred to Shanghai. Shortly after, I met my friend Mr. Yang again, and I told him that I had read *The Awakening of Faith* with great interest, but that frequently I came across philosophical terms which no existing dictionary explained, and which even excellent Chinese scholars could not explain. If he could spare some of his time to come to Shanghai, I would spare some of my time to translate it with his help. He readily agreed, and was delighted to have the book made known to those interested in Buddhism in the West. Thus the book was translated into English in 1894. But it was not published then, as I wished to have leisure time to revise it before publication. That time of leisure has never come. Six years later (1900), Suzuki's translation into English was published by the Open Court, Chicago. His translation bears the mark of one who has spent much study on the subject, but he did not possess the knowledge of the true key to the fundamental and central idea of the whole book, namely, Chen Jü. He translates it by "Suchness," which obscures his whole translation ; whereas I gave the literal translation True Model, meaning God, which later I found confirmed in an old standard Buddhist work called *Wan Fa Kwei Sin Luh*. In Suzuki's introduction, he quotes a large number of different authorities about Ashvagosha. But as he approaches the subject from the non-Christian point of view, the light which comes from a comparison between it and Christianity is denied him. He dwells more on his philosophical "suchness" or on his psychological theory of "triple personality" and only on one religious characteristic, "faith," apparently unconscious of its incalculable importance as a religious eirenicon between the East and the West. Though I have had no time to carefully revise this translation of mine, I publish it because I believe it is capable of producing brotherhood amongst men of different religions, when interpreted in the light of Christianity.

IV. Unity in Diversity

In the Chinese version of the Diamond Sutra, *Kin Kang King*, which is one of the most popular of all the Buddhist Sutras and most widely used throughout China, there is a very remarkable passage attributed to Gautama Buddha in the sixth chapter. It is to this effect: "Five hundred years after my death there will arise a religious prophet who will lay the foundation of his teaching, not on one, two, three, four, or five Buddhas, nor even on ten thousand Buddhas, but on the Fountain of all the Buddhas; when that One comes, have faith in Him, and you will receive incalculable blessings." Now, since it is well known that Jesus Christ and Ashvagosha did appear some five hundred years after Buddha, this is one of the most remarkable prophecies in the whole range of Sacred Literature.

But to return to *The Awakening of Faith*. It is of immense interest and importance to find in this book the following striking contrasts between the Old Buddhism and the New Buddhism.

1. The Old Buddhism was atheistic; the New is theistic.

2. The Old Buddhism trusted in salvation by one's own efforts (Karma); the New trusted in the help of God as well.

3. The Old Buddhism believed in retirement from the evil world; the New believed in living in the world and in saving others as the highest virtue.

4. The Old Buddhism believed in countless transmigrations before the many could be delivered; the New believed in passing into Paradise at once without any rounds of transmigration.

No one who is acquainted with the characteristics of Christianity can read these things without being struck with the remarkable similarity of these few points of the New Buddhism with it; nay, they are exactly the same so far as they go. Buddhism and Christianity at first contact in modern days were mutually hostile to one another. But when the earnest students of both religions penetrated through the different forms and nomenclature into the deep internal meaning of all, they found not only that they aimed at the same thing, the salvation of the world, but that many of their chief teachings were common to both. They no longer feared each other as foes, but helped each other as friends.

V. COMMON ORIGIN AROUND BABYLON

It is getting clearer each year now that these common doctrines of New Buddhism and Christianity were not borrowed from one another, but that both came from a common source, Babylonia, where some of the Jewish prophets wrote their glorious visions of the kingdom of God that was to come. Babylon then had much intercourse with Western India and Persia, as well as with Judea, Egypt, and Greece. From this centre these great life-giving, inspiring truths were carried like seeds into both the East and West, where they were somewhat modified under different conditions.

It is also getting clearer each year that different truths, wherever found, cannot be antagonistic. They do not neutralise, but complement each other; they do not destroy, but fulfil one another.

VI. ASHVAGOSHA

The various accounts of the life of Ashvagosha are so contradictory and many, so full of impossible

4

legends, that it is difficult to know how to separate the false from the true.   But all are agreed—

That he was a Brahman who was converted to Buddhism ;

That he travelled extensively in Central India and later in Northern India, and that he largely describes things of Western India in his book of Great Glory ;

That he was contemporary with, if not adviser of, a king, whose name is not yet quite known, of North-Western India, who lived in the first century of the Christian era.

That he was the founder of the New Buddhism, often called the Mahayana school, or the Northern Buddhism ;

That seven other works of his have been translated into Chinese, one of which is a celebrated life of Buddha translated by Beal.

His conversion as given by Suzuki is almost as striking as that which Yang related to me about his own conversion.   The day had come for a public discussion of religion, as was common in India at that time, and Ashvagosha and Pareva were to be the debaters.   Ashvagosha said, " The one unable to answer shall have his tongue cut out."   The other replied, " No, he shall become a disciple of the winner."   Then he asked Ashvagosha, " What shall we have to do in order to keep the kingdom in perfect peace, to have

the king live long, to let the people enjoy
abundance and prosperity, all free from evils
and catastrophes?" Not being able to answer
this, Ashvagosha became the other's disciple.

How to bring down high dogma to practical life
for the permanent good of all classes remains still
the great problem of life, philosophy, and religion.

VII. The Text

This book on *The Awakening of Faith* is mentioned in an old catalogue of Buddhist Scriptures in
the T'ang dynasty. I asked a friend in India to
try and procure me the copy of the original in
Sanskrit, but he has not succeeded. This Chinese
version of it was made by the Buddhist missionary
Paramartha, who lived in China in the Liang
dynasty, A.D. 502–555.

VIII. Translation

It is a common error of translators to translate
the same word always by the same word. As the
same word in different connections often has different
meanings, and the translated word, however literal,
does not always cover exactly the same amount of
meaning as the original, I have endeavoured to give
the true meaning of the original, although the English
rendering may be by different words in different

places. That is why I have rendered the term Chen Jü by True Form, True Model, True Reality, Archetype, and other terms, rather than by any unfamiliar term, as likely to give a more correct idea of the original to the student of Buddhism.

IX. Conclusion

The reader who is acquainted with the low state of Buddhism in China to-day may naturally ask, since the New Buddhism was so full of such high teaching on some of the greatest problems of life, and since it was so flourishing for many centuries, why is its glory departed ?   The answer is, besides what is given in Section II, that it is largely for want of proper education in its religion.   The same is true of Taoism.   It is only the Confucianists who have a grand system of education, and with that all power and influence is theirs, while the other religions have only reaped weakness and shame in consequence of their ignorance.   The term Julai, instead of being rendered by Tathagata, another foreign term, is best rendered by Messiah in English, as it literally means the "Model Come," *i.e.* the True Model become Incarnate.

TRANSLATOR'S SYNOPSIS

CHAPTER I

ANSWER. To give a comprehensive view of
the whole to intelligent men.

In the original state,
In the various states of acquired knowledge,
Behind thought and intermixed with the
  experience.
  (1) In this Original or Divine light
        there is—
    (*a*) Pure Wisdom,
    (*b*) Wonderful Goodness.
  (2) The attributes of this Original or
        Divine Light are—
    (*a*) Infinite recreation of the Eternal
          Unity as extensive as space
          and like a bright reflecting
          mirror.
    (*b*) Infinite Revelation of the Eternal
          Energy—a reflector of the
          real influences.
    (*c*) Infinite Revelation of Righteous
          Law—a reflector of that
          which is without sorrow or
          hindrance.
    (*d*) Infinite Revelation of Love—
          reflector which shines on all
          living beings.
  B. The Mahayana faith has acquired
        knowledge.   77
  (1) Producing three states of acquired
        knowledge—
    (*a*) Sensation,

(*b*) Consciousness,

(*c*) Perception.

Corresponding to a classification into six
stages of—   78

(*a*) Consciousness,

(*b*) Sensation,

(*c*) Perception,

(*d*) Differentiation,

(*e*) Will,

(*f*) Reflection.

(2) Showing two different conditions—   79
the Eternal and the Acquired.

(*a*) The same nature, just as a frag-
ment of pottery and all the
pottery are of clay.

(*b*) But different forms, just as the
clay is made into different
vessels.

(3) Producing the five kinds of
thoughts—

(*a*) Faculty of sensation,

(*b*)   „   consciousness,

(*c*)   „   perception,

(*d*)   „   conception,

(*e*)   „   will.

(4) Producing the opinions of imperfect knowledge.

Those ways which lead the soul astray are
six, namely—

(*a*) Through false perception,

(*b*) Through false affections,

(*c*) Through analogy of various knowledge,

(*d*) Through analogy of objective forms,

(*e*) Through inaccurate perception,

(*f*) Through inaccurate sensation.

(5) Having two states—the rough and the fine.

QUESTION 4. If the soul ends, how does it continue? If it continues, how does it end?   85

ANSWER. What ends is only the state of the soul, not the soul itself.

(6) Having four influences incessantly at work—the true, the untrue, the confused, the false objective.

(*a*) The misleading influence—

a.a. of the false world,

b.b. of false opinions,

c.c. of ignorance.

(*b*) The constant purifying influences—

a.a. of the imperfect good opinions,

b.b. of the transcendent.

(I) Directly by its own nature.

QUESTION 5. As all have the transcendent, PAGE
what need of faith and practice?   89

ANSWER. It is because imperfect knowledge
differs

      (II) Indirectly by the powers of other
          beings—

          (*a.a.a.*) Through different mo-
            tives,

          (*b.b.b.*) Through the same tran-
            scendent motives.

    (III) By contrast and by example.

      (*c*) One ends, the other never
        ends.

    (7) Having the Transcendent's own
      nature and state.

QUESTION 6. As the transcendent is independent of all states, how do you speak of all
kinds of blessings and possibilities?   93

ANSWER. Although it has these blessings,
it is independent of any state.

    (8) Having the transcendent in action
      —Buddha's vows begin here.

      (*a*) Has the faculty of distin-
        guishing between good
        and evil—the Regener-
        ated Spirit (Ying Shen).

      (*b*) Has the faculty of con-

scious indwelling — the
Inspired Spirit (Pao Shen).

(c) Has the faculty of knowing suffering.

(d) Has the faculty of perceiving the Divine Spirit (Fa Shên).

(e) Has finally the faculty beyond human experience —the Buddha experience.

QUESTION 7. If the Buddhas are independent of all visible states, how can they manifest themselves?   97

ANSWER. The spiritual state is the Soul of all the visible, therefore can manifest itself in the invisible.

(9) Being shown in leaving the immanent for the transcendent.

A. By correcting heresies

1. About terms such as

a. That Julai is space.

b. That nirvana and the transcendent are intangible.

c. That Julai embraces matter and spirit, therefore these cannot be cured.

QUESTION 8. As men and the transcendent
are the same, what need is there for practice ?

ANSWER. Like a precious stone from a
quarry, it must be polished.

QUESTION 9. To comprehend all beings in
all the worlds, how can any get this seed of
wisdom ?   109

ANSWER. By obtaining the omniscience that
is independent of the senses and is in all
minds.

QUESTION 10. If the Buddhas (Divine
Emanations) are incarnate everywhere to save
mankind, why do you say that most people
cannot see them ?   110

ANSWER. Only those pure like a bright
mirror are able to reflect and see such.

CHAPTER IV

III

THE AWAKENING OF FAITH

OPENING HYMN

I yield my life to the All,
To the ALL SOUL, full of good,
In wisdom all complete,
In power all divine,
In pity—would save all.

To LAW which does embody
The Archetype of all.

To CHURCH which does contain
The Archetype in Seed,

That men may be delivered
From doubt and evil ways;
Get Faith in the Great School
Perpetuating God!

CHAPTER I

REASONS FOR WRITING THE BOOK

QUESTION 1. What are the reasons for writing this book?

ANSWER. The reasons for it are eight—

A. Generally speaking, it is to induce all living

5

beings to depart from the way of all sorrow and to obtain the highest happiness, instead of seeking the glitter of fame and wealth of this world.

B. It is to make clear the fundamental idea of the incarnate God (Ju Lai) in man, and to lead all beings in the right way, avoiding error.

C. It is to lead those ripe in goodness to continue in the Mahayana Faith without failing.

D. It is to enable those in whom the root of goodness is very small to cultivate faith more and more.

E. It is to show how to remove evil hindrances and to strengthen well the mind, to keep far from mad pride, and to see through the deceits of vice.

F. It is to show how to study and correct the errors of ordinary men and the errors of the two inferior schools (the Hinayana or elementary school and the Madhyi-yana or middle school of Buddhism).

G. It is to show the means by which one may ascend to the abode of God (Buddha) and never lose faith.

H. It is to show the benefits of this Faith and to exhort men to practise it.

These are the main reasons for writing this book.

QUESTION 2. As the Sutras, or classic Buddhist Scriptures, explain these things fully, what need is there of repeating them ?

ANSWER. Although the Sutras have discussed these things, yet as men's abilities and attainments are different, the reception of instruction is necessarily different. When the incarnate God (Ju Lai) was on earth, all men were able to understand him. His body and mind far excelled those of all other men. When he delivered his perfect words, all living beings, though different in kind, understood him alike, and therefore there was no need of explanation.

But after Ju Lai's death we find that some men, after widely reading our Sacred Scriptures, have the power unaided to understand them; we find that others, after only hearing a little of the Sacred Scriptures, have the power unaided to understand much; we also find that some have not sufficient intelligence to understand the Scriptures unassisted by extensive explanations; whilst we find that others dislike voluminous writings and prefer a terse style which embraces many principles, and which they are able to understand.

Thus this book is written for the last class of men which desire to know the general principles of the great and profound Law of Ju Lai with its infinite applications.

CHAPTER II

The Fundamental Doctrine of the Mahayana Faith

Having explained the object of writing this book, we now proceed to consider the fundamental doctrine of the Mahayana Faith. The great school (Mahayana) speaks of the Eternal Soul of the universe, His nature and His attributes.

A. By His nature is meant the Soul of all living beings. The soul embraces that of saved and of unsaved beings, and it is this universal Soul that characterises the great school. For it is the Archetype's True Eternal Form which is the nature of the Mahayana Faith; and the Archetype's temporory form in life which is able to make manifest the nature, form, and use of the Mahayana Faith.

B. As to the attributes of this Soul, they are three. The first is the vastness of its nature. All things are originally one and the same and an eternally fixed quantity in the True Model. The second covers its vast manifestations. In the person of Ju Lai, the True Model Come, there are infinite possibilities stored up as in a womb. The third is its vast power. It is able to produce all good among all classes of unsaved beings.

All the enlightened Buddhas follow this Mahayana Faith, and all the chief saints (Pusas) attain to the perfection of Ju Lai by the methods of this Faith of the New Buddhism.

CHAPTER III

Expositions of the Mahayana Faith

These expositions are of three kinds—

A. Those about the meaning.

B. Those about the correction of erroneous conceptions.

C. Those about the different steps of progress.

As to the meaning of the One Soul, there are two aspects—

1. One is the eternal transcendent Soul.

2. The other is the temporary immanent Soul.

These two aspects embrace everything, for they are really one.

1. The eternal state of the Soul.

The Soul or Mind of the True Model is the great essence of the invisible and the visible worlds.   As to the nature of this One Soul, it is the same in all forms.   To think it is different in different forms is only a false notion of the world.   Once we penetrate beyond forms, it is discovered that all the different forms of the universe are not real differences of soul at all, but different manifestations of one real power, hence it has always been impossible to speak adequately, to name correctly, or to think correctly of this One Soul, the real essence of things, which is unchangeable and indestructible. We therefore name it the TRUE ESSENCE OR THE TRUE LIKENESS OR THE TRUE FORM OR MODEL. But all nomenclature of these matters is imperfect, and if one follows superficial thought, the true meaning cannot be found out. Even though we call it the True Model, it has no form. It is because language in its extremity fails us that we coin a new term to avoid ordinary ideas. But the nature of this Archetype is a reality that cannot be destroyed, for all things are true though they cannot be truly pointed out to the senses, and all forms are really only different manifestations of the one True Model. It should be remembered that this is beyond ordinary language and beyond ordinary thought, therefore we name it the True Model.

QUESTION 3. How then are men to follow and obey and find the way to this True Model of things ?

ANSWER. One must know that although one cannot speak of this adequately, as it is beyond all expression, and although one cannot think of this adequately, as it is beyond all thought, yet we call this state the seeking after ; and that when we leave ordinary thought of these things, we are entering into the gate of knowledge. Next, when using words to discuss the True Model, it may be spoken of in two ways, namely, first as the unreal as compared with ordinary realities, in order eventually to show its reality ; secondly, as the only real as compared with ordinary realities, because it has a nature of its own full of infinite possibilities.

A. *First, then, the Unreal.*

When we speak of the unreal, we mean that which has never been defined, which is separate from all existing forms, and which common men cannot understand.

We should know the nature of this True Model. It has no form, yet it is not formless. This is not saying that it is without any form, but that it is not the ordinary form. It is composed of neither ordinary, existing, nor non-existing forms. It is neither one definite form nor is it the many different forms. This is not saying that it has no definite form and that it is not in the many different forms. It is neither one nor many different forms. Generally speaking, as the world has many different notions, all false, we call this the Unreal Empty Form. But if false notions are given up, this is then the most Real.

B. *Secondly, the Real.*

When we speak of the Real, we have already explained that the True Form is apparently Unreal but true; in other words, that it is the true mind, eternal, and unchanged, full of purity, therefore we call it the Real One. But it has no form. When the imperfect notions of things are given up, then alone can we verify this truth.

2. The Eternal Soul immanent in the temporary.

The temporary arises from the forces of the Eternal Ju Lai, the uniting of the eternal with the temporary. It is neither the same nor different, but we call it the Natural state of man. This natural state has two meanings, namely, that which embraces all things, and that which produces all things : the first is called the Infinite Enlightenment, the second the Finite Enlightenment.

A. *Infinite Enlightenment.*

By infinite enlightenment is meant that which has no false notions and is infinite like space, one with the True Form, as in instinct and intuition. This is the natural state of the Incarnate True Model (Ju Lai), and is called the original state of enlightenment. This is to distinguish it from acquired enlightenment, which cultivates that infinite enlightenment, for the two have the same thing in common though it is only in part. Where there is the original infinite enlightenment there exists finite enlightenment in those who seek after it. Where there exists finite enlightenment, there is more enlightenment to be acquired.

Again, when one attains to the original enlightenment, it is called the perfect enlightenment. When one has not attained to the original enlightenment, it is not perfect enlightenment.

For example, when an ordinary man discovers that his former ideas were wrong, and is able to prevent such ideas arising any more, such knowledge on his part, though it might be called a kind of enlightenment, is only finite.

Or when those learned in the wisdom of the two lower schools (the primary and secondary, or smaller and middle), or such Pusa saints as are beginners in the Mahayana school are enlightened so as to know that there is in one sense a difference and in another no difference between these two classes of ideas, we call their knowledge partial enlightenment.

Or when those, such as the saints who have arrived at different stages of attainment, are enlightened to know that there is in one sense a resting-place and in another sense no rest, in order to distinguish things more clearly, their knowledge is called partial enlightenment.

Or when the saints have arrived at the highest attainment with all the means of deliverance completed and their thoughts exactly in accordance with the original enlightenment, and are enlightened to know that when the false notions began, these had no real beginning; yet, in order to escape far from microscopic anxious thought of things, they are able to see the true nature of the

One Mind. This state is the eternal one which we call the perfect enlightenment. Therefore the Sutra says that when one can apprehend that which is behind thought, one is on the way to Buddhist wisdom !

Again, as to the beginning of imperfect notions in the mind of men, these have no beginning. But when we speak of their beginning, we mean that they arise without thought, therefore are not called enlightened, as they have not exercised thought. As each thought has been transmitted without interruption from the beginning, and men's minds have not been able to free themselves from this, the imperfect notions have been said to be without beginning and to be finite enlightenment. If we meet a man without these thoughts, we shall then know the different stages in the development of the mind, such as beginning, resting satisfied, considering, ending, because without thought he knows that there is really no difference in kind between the enlightened neophyte's enlightenment and the original enlightenment. For the four states are co-existent and not independent, but are originally all alike—different stages of one and the same enlightenment.

(1) Next, original enlightenment in men appears according to the different degrees of confusion in two different states, but not separate from the original enlightenment. These different states are

the state of pure wisdom and the state of
unspeakable blessing where things are incomprehensible.

(*a*) The state of pure wisdom is that which exists
when, under the transforming influence of the True
Model, cultivating one's nature according to the
True Model till all departments of deliverance are
completed, when one reaches the state where the
temporary gives way to the eternal and is grafted on
to the Eternal Mind, manifesting itself in the three
spiritual institutions—of Buddha (Godhead), of Law,
and of Priesthood, hence called the perfect and pure
wisdom, because all who are dependent on the senses
alone are unenlightened.   Those in the unenlightened state do not depart from the nature of
enlightenment; they are neither destructible so
long as they depend on the original enlightenment
nor indestructible when independent of that.   Just
as the water in the ocean, on account of wind,
forms itself into waves, wind and waves being
inseparable, and yet motion is not an attribute of
water (for if the wind ceases the waves also cease),
but the fluid nature of water remains indestructible ;
so the true nature of man is a clear pure mind.
Though on account of the rise of the wind of finite
enlightenment the pure mind is moved, the pure
mind and the finite knowledge in man's heart are
unseen and inseparable, but this mind's nature is not
finite enlightenment.   If the finite enlightenment

ceases, then the imperfect notions will cease, and
the wise nature remains indestructible.

(*b*) The state of unspeakable blessing is the
practical, when it follows pure wisdom and is able
to do all sorts of wonderful things, being called the
state of infinite blessings, unceasing and natural.
In proportion to the natural goodness it abounds in
all kinds of blessings according to the need of all.

(2) Next consider the attributes of this enlightenment. They are four great ones, infinite
as space and clear as a mirror.

(*a*) Infinite light of the Eternal (Real Emptiness).
It is very different from all thought and form. It
cannot be made apparent and enlightenment cannot
reveal it to the unenlightened.

(*b*) Infinite light of energy which influences
things and which is called the unseen forces (not
Real Emptiness). All appearances in the world
are brought about by this. They are without
appearing and disappearing, without loss or de-
struction, eternal in the One Mind. All existence
is but the true nature of this Mind. Moreover,
all kinds of defilement cannot defile this. Its
nature of wisdom is unchanged, full of perfect
energy, influencing all men.

(*c*) Infinite light of the law of deliverance called
the invariable law of Salvation (not Unreal Law),
which sets aside the hindrances of pessimism and
the hindrances to ordinary wisdom and leads one

out of the state where the mortal and the immortal are combined so as to get into the perfect free light of life.

(*d*) The infinite light of practice, called deliverance according to the law, shining on the minds of all living beings, leading them to practise goodness by methods suitable to their needs.

B. *Finite Enlightenment or Acquired Knowledge.*

This is not like the knowledge of the Eternal that there is only one way : hence finite enlightenment shows itself in many forms of existence. These forms have no independent existence separated from the original enlightenment. Just as with a man who has lost his way, his losing of the way depends on his original knowledge of his course (for if he had no idea of the way at first, he could not be said to have lost it), so with men, it is because they have the idea of enlightenment that they know they are unenlightened. If they had no idea of enlightenment in the abstract, they could not be said to be altogether unenlightened. From imperfect ideas of unenlightenment men are able to understand the meaning of words and true enlightenment. If we dispense with finite enlightenment, we cannot conceive of true enlightenment.

(1) First, finite enlightenment may be viewed in three ways always inseparable from it—

(*a*) Sensation. When the unenlightened mind

is excited we call it sensation. When there is enlightenment there is no excitement; if there is excitement there is pain, as effect follows cause.

(b) Consciousness. This occurs when following any excitement one becomes conscious of something. Without sensation there is no consciousness.

(c) Perception. This is formed when following consciousness the external becomes real. Without consciousness there are no perceptions of outside objects.

Since there is an objective world, there arise again six aspects of it according to another classification, namely—

(a) Consciousness, which arises from outward objects which the mind distinguishes between one and another—between what it likes and what it dislikes.

(b) Emotion. This follows consciousness and produces joy and sorrow. These false ideas arise from constant partial enlightenment.

(c) Attention. This follows emotion, reaching after everything, seizing on joy and sorrow and cleaving to them with the whole mind.

(d) Conception. This follows perception, distinguishing it by giving it a name.

(e) Will. This follows the giving of names to things in all sorts of action.

(f) Discrimination. This is the result of different action, and is inevitable. We should know that unenlightenment can produce all kinds of false methods, because they are within the state of unenlightenment.

(2) Next, infinite enlightenment and finite enlightenment may be viewed together in two ways, namely, where they are the same and where they are different.

(a) As to where they are the same. Take, for example, the various kinds of pottery : they are all made of one clay. In the same way finite enlightenments are manifestations of the One True Essence, and the Sutras according to this doctrine say that all things are eternal and divine. Perfect enlightenment cannot be cultivated or made, can never be added to, and has no form which can be seen. That which has form to be seen accompanies useful transformations. It is not the nature of real Wisdom, for this Wisdom is invisible.

(b) As to where enlightenment and unenlightenment differ, it is like speaking of the different kinds of pots made. Infinite enlightenment and finite enlightenment differ according to their useful transformations, and the infinite nature appears different in the transformations.

(3) Next, the finite forces which control human nature, such as the changes of mind and consciousness, arise from ignorance and unenlightenment. They may be seen manifested in our feelings and spoken of as mental powers. These mental powers

have five names. One is the faculty exercised
when in the midst of ignorance finite consciousness
begins. The second is the faculty used when the
mind takes note of something. The third is the
faculty used when all phenomena are put in the
objective. Just as outward things are reflected
in a mirror, so does this faculty reflect what the
five senses show instantaneously at all times. The
fourth is the faculty used when distinguishing
between the pure and impure. The fifth is the
faculty used when it reflects impressions from one
object to the other incessantly. It retains the
past infinite manifestations of one's own existence
with all their good and evil; it ripens into the
knowledge of the causes of present and future
joy and sorrow which are the unfailing results of
our deeds; it is able to call up the past, lay it
instantly before our mind and to call up our
finite knowledge of the future. Therefore the
phenomena of the three worlds (of desire, of form,
and of no form) are mind-made. Without mind,
then, there is practically no objective existence.
Thus all existence arises from imperfect notions
of our mind. All differences are differences of
the mind. But the mind cannot see itself, for
it has no form. We should know that all
phenomena are created by the imperfect notions
of the finite mind, therefore all existence is like
a reflection in a mirror, without substance, only

a phantom of the mind. When the finite mind acts, then all kinds of things arise; when the finite mind ceases to act, then all kinds of things cease.

Next, the faculty of thought. This comes out of the fifth as above. In common men this is very strong. The consciousness of self and of environment and all the imperfect ideas arising from these, trying to distinguish between all the objects of the senses, is called thought, and is also called the independent faculty, as well as the faculty of distinguishing things. This increases with the senses, with desires, and with their sorrows.

(4) As to the origin of imperfect knowledge working in the finite, common men cannot understand this; nor can the wisdom of the two lower schools understand it; only the Pusa saints of Higher Buddhism, when they begin to get right faith, and when they can examine things properly and test the nature of the True Model, can understand it. Spiritual men can get a small insight into this; but even the higher saints when they have attained to their perfect state cannot understand the whole of it. Only Buddha (God) understands all. The mind from the beginning is of a pure nature, but since there is the finite aspect of it which is sullied by finite views, there is the sullied aspect of it. Although there is this defilement, yet the original pure nature is

6

eternally unchanged.   This mystery only Buddha understands.

When we speak of the original nature of the mind, eternally without thought, we call it eternally unchanged.   As the human mind originally does not know the True Model, the mind does not correspond with the outward universe.   Then thought suddenly begins and is called the finite thought.

Confusion from correspondence with the objective. One can be delivered from this confusion by the two lower schools and be kept far from it in the station of full faith of the great school.   Confusion arises through feeling corresponding with the objective.   One can gradually avoid this by the cultivation of the means of deliverance in the full faith of the great school; by the cultivation to the First station in the pure state of the mind, all the confusion will be gone.   (To understand these and the stations below, see *Guide to Buddhahood*, translated by the Author.)

Confusion through knowledge of differences by correspondence with the objective.   By means of the second stage of separateness from the world, and by means of deliverance in the Seventh station, confusion will be gone.

Confusion through objective forms not corresponding with one another.   By means of the Eighth station of freedom from form (or the immovable) all the confusion will be gone.

Confusion through subjective perception not corresponding with the objective. By means of the Ninth station, when the mind is free (in holy wisdom) the confusion can be got rid of.

Confusion through subjective sensation not corresponding with the objective. By means of the complete ten stations of the saints one may enter the state of Ju Lai, Buddhahood, and be delivered from this last of the confusions. As the finite mind does not comprehend the universal Soul, it begins by the correspondence of faith to examine into things and to rid itself of confusion. In its progress towards purity of mind, it step by step gets rid of confusion, and when it arrives at the state of Ju Lai, it is able to be free from it altogether.

The meaning of correspondence is that the finite mind's ideas of the universal True Form differ according to their stages of confusion or enlightenment, and that the perfected finite knowledge and the outside universe are exactly the same. The meaning of want of correspondence is that the finite mind is unenlightened and has never known these differences, and that its knowledge and the outside universe are not the same.

Again, the confused mind is a hindrance to thought and darkens the original wisdom of the True Model. Ignorance is called the hindrance of wisdom, and darkens the natural wisdom of the world. What does this mean? It means that, owing to the confused mind, its perceptions, its objects and thoughts are not in accordance with the Eternal Nature. It means that, owing to the universal True Form being eternally at rest, without being finite or temporary, ignorance and unenlightenment differ from the eternal, therefore they are unable to follow the perfect wisdom of all the universe.

(5) Next the finite state. This is of two kinds. First, the rough ordinary state when it corresponds with the finite mind. Second, the fine extra-ordinary state when it does not correspond with the finite mind. There is also the lowest of the ordinary, such as the state of common men, and the highest of the ordinary. There is, too, the lowest of the extraordinary, such as the state of the Pusa saints; and the highest of the extraordinary, such as the state of Buddha. These two kinds of the finite state arise from the different extent of the influence of ignorance. As to cause and effect, the cause is unenlightenment, the effect is the manufacture of a false imperfect world. If the cause is removed, then the effect is removed. If the imperfect cause ceases, then the imperfect mind which does not correspond with the real universe also ceases. If the result ceases to be erroneous, then the mind which corresponds with the real universe also ceases to be erroneous.

QUESTION 4. If the finite mind ceases, how can there be continuation? If there be continuation, how then do you speak of finally ceasing altogether?

ANSWER. What is destroyed is only the finite state of the mind, not the mind's being, just as wind in relation to water is a moving power. If there be no water, the effect of the wind is not apparent; there is nothing to show it. If the water remains, the state of the wind is made apparent; only when the wind ceases does the moving of the water cease. It is not the water that ceases to exist. So ignorance in relation to the True Real Nature is made apparent.

If there were no True Real Nature of the mind, then all existence would not exist; there would be nothing to show it. If the True Real Nature of the mind remains, then finite mind continues. Only when the madness of finite mind ceases will the finite mind cease. It is not the wisdom of the True Reality that ceases.

(6) Influences. There are four influences—the confused and the pure—incessantly at work. The first is a pure influence called the True Real One. The second is the cause of all confusion, called ignorance. The third is the confused mind, called sensation. The fourth is the false world as known to the senses and called the objective.

Influences may be thus illustrated. Clothes have no scent, but if any one smoked them with incense, the clothes would then be perfumed like the incense. So it is with influences. The True Reality is pure and has really no confusion colouring it, but ignorance in man colours his views, so that there is a confused state. The confusion caused by ignorance has really no true purity, but the True Reality influences the mind, so that there is an effort after the true purity.

(a) How is it that confused influences are acting incessantly? It is in relation to the True Model that there is ignorance as a cause of the confusion. This ignorance colours the True Model in the finite mind. As there is an influence at work, there arise false imperfect ideas, and these colour the True Model again so that one does not understand it. Unenlightenment then arises, bringing a new world of false conceptions on account of this result. These false ideas in turn colour other false conceptions again, causing the mind to be fixed on these and to desire to do all sorts of things, incurring thus all kinds of trouble of both mind and body.

a.a. The influences of the false objective world are of two kinds, namely, those which arise from increased thought, and those which arise from increased action.

b.b. The influences of the false imperfection of

faculties are of two kinds, namely, those which arise
voluntarily from faculties producing the highest
saints of the lower school (the Hinayana), the
highest saints of the middle school, and the highest
saints (the Pusas) of the advanced school (the
Mahayana), causing them to suffer the sorrows
of life and change; and those which arise involun-
tarily from faculties producing ordinary men and
causing them to suffer the sorrows of successive
transmigrations.

c.c. The influences of ignorance are of two kinds:
first, those which arise from the very root of things
—intuition—which give rise to imperfect sensation; and second, those which arise from the senses
and desires, and which give rise to imperfect
impressions.

(*b*) How is it that pure influences are acting
incessantly? It is because there is a True Model
able to influence the ignorant, a power at work
causing man's misguided mind to dislike the sorrows
of transmigration and to seek the joys of divine
rest (nirvana). As this ignorant mind is moved to
dislike transmigration and love nirvana, this fact
influences the finite mind to believe that its nature
is finite and to know that its finite mind is full of
false ideas; and further, that there is no true
objective world before men, and that therefore they
are to cultivate some way of deliverance. As from
the True Model man knows that there is no

objective world, then the various means of following and obeying this True Model arise spontaneously (without thought and without action); and when influenced by this power for a long time, ignorance disappears. As ignorance disappears, then false ideas cease to arise. As these false ideas do not arise, the former objective world also ends. As the forces cease to exist, then the false powers of the finite mind cease to exist, and this is called NIR-VANA, when the natural forces of the True Model alone work.

a.a. The influence of the imperfect mind is of two kinds, namely, that which arises from positiveness and literalness, as in common men and in those of the two lower schools, causing them to dislike the rounds of transmigration and, according to their strength, to gradually move towards the unsurpassed way of Buddhism; and that which arises from the five faculties of the mind, where the higher saints start to copy the True Model to reach nirvana quickly.

b.b. The influence of the True Model, which is of two kinds, namely. that which arises from subjective influences of the True Model element itself, and that which arises from outward conditions.

a.a. The influence of the True Model itself is from eternal ages, having infinite resources complete with benefits beyond all thought. It underlies the nature of all phenomena.

On account of this twofold aspect the power of

these influences is unceasing, causing all men to dislike the sorrows of transmigration and seek the joys of nirvana, believing that in their own persons there is the influence of the True Model, and that therefore they have a mind to cultivate it.

QUESTION 5. If this be so, that all living beings have the True Model in them, and that all will be equally influenced, why should there be the infinite distinction of believing and unbelieving, some first and others later? Should not all at the same time know the power of the True Model, causing them to diligently cultivate the means of deliverance, and enabling all to enter nirvana?

ANSWER. The True Model is originally only one, but the degrees of ignorance are infinite, therefore the natures of men differ in character accordingly. There are unruly thoughts more numerous than the sands of the Ganges, some arising from ignorant conceptions and others arising from ignorance of senses and desires. Thus all kinds of wild thoughts arise from ignorance, and have first and last infinite differences which Ju Lai alone knows.

Again, in the method of all the Buddhas there are means of utilising their forces. The nature and the means must be at work to be complete. Just as wood, though it has fire latent in it (this fire being the real force), cannot burn unless men know this and use means to call it forth, so with men

although there is the power of the influence of the
True Model in them, if it does not meet with the
noble forces of the Buddhas and Pusas as a means
to call it forth, there would be no means of preventing wild thoughts and of entering nirvana.
And although there would be the force of outward
conditions, yet without the influence of the True
Model there would not be the power by which one
could discard the sorrows of transmigration and
seek the joys of nirvana.

If the forces and the means of utilising them
are complete, such as the force of the influences of
the True Model and also of the loving vows
of the perfected Buddhas and of the almost
perfect saints to save the world, there arises
a dislike to sorrow and a belief in nirvana
and the cultivation of a good character. When
the good character is attained, such people find
the Buddhas and Pusas teaching them directly the
benefits and the joys of the doctrine, and they are
able to enter into the way of nirvana.

b.b. The influence of outward conditions. This
is the power of outward forces, and these outward
conditions are incalculable. We indicate two kinds,
those of different methods and those of the same
spirit.

a.a.a. As to the influences of different methods,
they are those which operate when men follow the
Buddhas and the Pusas from the beginning of their

desire to seek truth till they themselves become
Buddhas, and which influence them all through
their course, be it in what they see or think,
whether through their own family, parents, or
relatives, or through servants, or dear friends, or
through enemies, or by means of the four attractions (such as those caused by alms, kind words,
help and sharing in toil), even including all sorts of
incalculable means, in order to set in action the
power of the loving influences of the Buddhas and
Pusas, so as to induce all beings to increase in
goodness and benefit by what they see or hear.
These means are also of two kinds, namely, the
direct, which enables one to get saved quickly ; and
the indirect, which enables one to get saved after
a longer time.   The direct and indirect means are
again of two kinds, namely, the progressive practice
and the final attainment.

b.b.b. As to influences of the same spirit, all the
Buddhas and Pusas desire to deliver all men from
sorrow, and these spirits influence men constantly
without ceasing, and they are of the same nature
and wisdom and power, therefore manifest the same
spirit in all their experience.   This is experienced
when men in their ecstasy are able to see the
Buddhas.

c.c. The difference between the influences of the
True Model is of two kinds.   The first is the un-
corresponding.   It is that of the common man or

of the two lower schools and first stages of the
Great School. These are influenced by their
consciousness and impression, but are able to
improve by means of the power of faith. They
have not attained to that correspondence of mind
with the Absolute whereby they are one with the
nature of the True Model, and have not attained
that experience which is natural and perfectly
corresponding to the work of the True Model.

The second is the corresponding. It is that of
the perfected Buddhas who have attained to the
state when their mind is not different from that of
the True Model, but corresponding to the nature
and work of all the Buddhas. In this state men
are able to act naturally by means of the power of
the Absolute Spirituality, and by the influence of
the Absolute to put an end to ignorance.

(c) Next note the confused state.

The influence of this confused state has been
going on from eternity without ceasing, but when
one reaches the state of Buddhahood this ceases.
But the influence of the pure state has no end; it
has for ever a future! It is the influence of the
Absolute Reality. The confused idea is ended and
the spiritual is manifested in the influence it exerts
on work and has no end.

(7) As to the nature and state of the Absolute, that of all common men, that of the lower
school, that of the middle school, that of the

advanced, and that of the Buddhas are without
a difference, only having more or less of it. It
is neither that which had an origin some time, nor
that which will end at some time; it is really
eternal. In its nature it is always full of all
possibilities, and is described as of great light
and wisdom, giving light to all things, real and
knowing. Its true nature is that of a pure mind,
eternally joyful, the true soul of things, pure, quiet,
unchanged, therefore free with fulness of virtues
and attributes of Buddha more numerous than
the sands of the Ganges; divine, unending, unchanged, and unspeakable. It is most complete,
without lacking anything, it is called the treasury or
storehouse or womb of Ju Lai (the Model Come),
and also the Divine Body of Ju Lai.

QUESTION 6. Now you have said above that the
nature of the Absolute is the same in all beings and
is apart from all forms, how is it that you speak of its
nature as having all these different possibilities ?

ANSWER. Although real and possessing these
possibilities, yet they are not different qualities;
they are of one kind only, one Absolute Reality;
there is a likeness in all the different manifestations, therefore they cannot be different. Again,
how do we say that there is a difference ? It is
in relation to consciousness and the finite that this
difference appears. And how does it appear ? As

regards the origin of all things there is but One Mind, not an unenlightened Mind conjecturing at things, for in the finite there are imperfect ideas. The unenlightened mind begins to think of the world around, and this we call ignorance. If this finite thought conjecturing at things had not arisen, there would have been great wisdom and light. When the human mind begins to see that there exists the unseen beyond, where the mind nature is independent of this seeing, then it finds that this unseen shines throughout the universe. If the mind is excited or prejudiced, the knowledge is not true knowledge. When it has not found its true nature, it is not eternal, not joyful, not the true soul of things, not pure, but is busy and decaying, and therefore not free, and thus full of confusion more numerous than the sands of the Ganges. On the other hand, if the mind is not excited or prejudiced by imperfect ideas, all sorts of pure possibilities more numerous than the sands of the Ganges are open to it. If in the human mind there arises an idea to be followed, it is because there is something lacking in the mind. Thus the incalculable possibilities of the pure Absolute Nature is that of the One Mind. There is no need to think out any new idea; it is complete, and is called the divine state, the treasury or storehouse or womb of Ju Lai.

(8) As to the work of the True Model—it is

that which is in all the Buddhas and Ju Lai from
that first moment of great love and desire to
cultivate their own salvation and then to save
others, to the time of their great vow to save all
beings throughout all future endless kalpas. They
regard all living beings as their own selves, though
they are not the same in form, for in reality all
living beings and themselves are manifestations of
the Absolute Reality without any difference; then
with the aid of this great wisdom of the True
Model they put an end to ignorance, they see the
divine, and there arise naturally all sorts of un-
imaginable service like that of the Absolute Reality
reaching everywhere. Yet these beings are not
ordinary forms, for the Buddhas and Ju Lai are
perfect embodiments of the divine. The chief thought
is that they are not the ordinary ideas of the world;
they are not ordinary workers, but such workers
as influence or inspire people in their experiences,
hence we say they are the work of the True Model.

(a) This spiritual work of the True Model is of
two kinds. The first is dependent on the senses
(positive and literal) and on what the mind of
the ordinary man and those of the two lower
schools understand by them, hence this kind is
called the common stage, as these people do not
know that their work is the manifestation of their
sensation, so regard it outwardly by colour and size,
but do not fully know.

(*b*) The second is dependent on the faculties. It is what all the Pusas from the time they reach the first station till they reach the highest station have experienced, and is called the inspired stage (Pao Shen). This stage has incalculable manifestations ; these manifestations have incalculable states, and these states have incalculable blessings.

The results of this stage have also all kinds of incalculable glories according to their manifestations. They are endless and infinite, without measure, ever present in their reactions, indestructible, and never lost. These blessings are the results of the perfect influences of the six means of salvation (Paramita or Wisdoms) and of the transcendent influences of the Absolute Reality. Thus the Pusa saints are full of immeasurable joy, hence they are called the inspired spirits.

(*c*) As to what common men see, it is only the rough outline. These men according to their observations see all sorts of different living creatures in the six kinds of beings (gods, men, ashuras, devils, hungry ghosts, beasts); they have not attained the state of joy, hence they are called common spirits.

(*d*) As to what the Pusa saints know from the beginning of their free ideas, and what begins to appear to them by full faith in the True Model, they know some of its characteristics, and glory that they are ever present, immeasurable, only manifest in the mind, and inseparable from the Absolute Reality. But these Pusas still have some imperfect notions remaining, as they have not reached the full Divine State. If they reach a purer state of mind, and if they progress till they have reached the utmost state, the inspired is seen to perfection.

(e) When they pass beyond the sense and faculties, there is no visible state, for the Divine Soul of all the Buddhas has no outward form by which they are to be seen.

QUESTION 7. If the Divine Spirit of all the Buddhas is separated from form, how can it manifest any forms?

ANSWER. This Divine Soul is the essence of all form, therefore it can manifest itself in form. This is why we say mind and matter are eternally the same. As the essence of matter is WISDOM, the essence of matter is without form and is called the embodiment of wisdom. As the manifested essence of wisdom is matter, it is called the all-pervading embodiment of wisdom. The unmanifested matter is without magnitude; according to the will, it can show itself throughout all the universe as the immeasurable Pusas, immeasurable inspired spirits, immeasurable glories, all different, without magnitude and without interference with one another. This is what ordinary senses cannot

7

comprehend, as it is the work of the True Model (Absolute Reality).

(9) Now we show how to proceed from the finite to the infinite. This is called analysing all experience of matter to mind. In all the six objects of sense there does not exist false conjectures as men's thoughts are. As the mind has no form, we seek for it at all points of space in vain. Just as a man having lost his way calls the east west, although the east and west have not really changed, so is mankind lost in ignorance, calling the mind of the universe his thoughts! But the Mind is what it ever was, all unchanged by men's thought. When men consider and realise that the Absolute Mind has no need of thoughts like men, they are then following the right way to reach the Infinite.

B. The rectification of erroneous conceptions. All kinds of erroneous conceptions arise from our own conceptions of things. If we could put away these personal conceptions, there would then be no false ones. These personal conceptions are of two kinds, namely, false conceptions of the person as the self, anthropomorphically, and false conceptions arising from that.

1. That which regards personal being as self.

According to common language, it is of five kinds—

a. Hearing the Sutras saying that the eternal nature of Ju Lai is in the end only vacuity like space, some men, not knowing that this expression was used in order to destroy belief in phenomena as real, say that Space or Emptiness itself is Ju Lai. How is this to be rectified? Men are to understand that space is nothing. It has no existence and is not a reality. It is a term in opposition to reality. We only say this or that is visible in order that we might distinguish between things. All phenomena are originally in the Mind and have really no outward form, therefore as there is no form it is a mistake to think there is anything there. All phenomena only arise from false notions of the Mind. If the Mind is independent of these false ideas, then all phenomena disappear. This is called the true glorious nature and wisdom of Ju Lai, the Model Come (manifested), and not mere empty space.

b. Hearing the Sutras saying that the nature of all things in the world is unreal, even the final nature of nirvana and of the True Model (the Absolute Reality), therefore they are also intangible and eternally independent of all forms, some men, not knowing that it was for the purpose of destroying belief in phenomena that these expressions were used, say the nature of the True Model and nirvana is nothing but unreality. How is this to be rectified? They are to understand that the divine nature of the True Model is not unreal. It is full of infinite possibilities.

c. Hearing the Sutras saying that the treasures

of Ju Lai (the Manifested Model) are eternally
fixed without addition or subtraction, and are
potentially full of all possibilities, some men, not
understanding it, say the treasures of Ju Lai
contain both the distinctions of mind and matter.
How is this to be rectified? According to the
True Model, there is no distinction between mind
and matter; it is on account of the defilement of
the finite in the round of life and death that these
distinctions appear.

d. Hearing the Sutras saying that all the defilements of life and death exist because they are in
the treasury of Ju Lai, as nothing is independent
of the True Model, some men, not understanding
it, say the attributes of Ju Lai originally contain
everything that there is in the world pertaining to
life and death. How is this to be rectified? As
the attributes of Ju Lai from eternity only contain
pure possibilities more numerous than the sands of
the Ganges, they are not independent of the True
Model. They never fail, and are not different from
the True Model. As to the defilements of the
world, they are all false; they have no reality
behind them. From eternity they have had nothing in them corresponding to Ju Lai. If there
had been defilement in the nature of Ju Lai's
attributes, to get rid of defilement by causing men
to unite with Ju Lai would be an absurdity.

e. Hearing the Sutras saying that life and death

depend on the treasures of Ju Lai, and that nirvana also depends on the treasures of Ju Lai, some men, not understanding it, say that all beings have a beginning, and as they have a beginning they then say that the joys of nirvana which Ju Lai has obtained have an end when he comes again incarnate. How is this to be rectified? As the treasures of Ju Lai are without a beginning, so is the state of ignorance without a beginning. If it be said that beyond the three worlds—earth, heaven, and hell, or form, desire, and no-form—there are other beings, this is but the talk of non-Buddhist Scriptures. Moreover, as the treasures of Ju Lai are without an end, so is nirvana, which all the Buddhas obtain, without end.

2. To meet the intelligent of the two lower schools, Ju Lai only spoke to them of the True Model as not like men (not anthropomorphic). As he had not spoken fully to them of the temporary nature of experience, they feared the rounds of life and death and sought a false nirvana. How is this to be rectified? As the nature behind all experience has no beginning, so it has no end— this is the true nirvana.

3. Finally, to leave false conceptions, one should know that purity and defilement are both relative terms and have no independent existence. Although all things from eternity are neither matter nor mind, neither infinite wisdom nor finite knowledge,

neither existing nor non-existing, but are after all inexpressible, we nevertheless use words, yet should know that Ju Lai's skilful use of words to lead men aright lay in this—to get men to cease conjecturing and to return to the Absolute Reality, for the best human thought of all things is only temporary and is not Absolute truth.

C. Different steps of progress. These are the paths which all the Buddhas have passed through, and the goals reached by the Pusas when they have made up their minds to practise religion. Briefly speaking, religious growth or progress involves having three things: first, growth of perfect faith; second, growth in intelligent practice; third, growth in attainments.

1. The progress of perfect faith. It depends on the kind of man, and the kind of character he has, whether he gets a perfect faith worthy of progress. This again depends on uncertainty of character, whether tending to good or evil. If influenced by goodness, believing that good and evil have their respective recompense, if able to abound in all sorts of good works, if tired with the sorrows of life and death, if desiring to obtain the highest wisdom by meeting all the Buddhas and by worshipping and supporting them in person and practising faith long under all conditions, then faith is perfect, and the Buddhas and Pusas teach such how to progress. Some, moved by great pity, are able to progress of

themselves ; others, on seeing the right doctrine about to be attacked, are moved to defend it.   Such persons are able to progress.   Thus, when faith is perfect and the religious aim is fixed, they enter the ranks of the upright and true fixed ones ; they never go back, and are reckoned among the seed of the children of Ju Lai, being one with the right eternal Cause of things.

a. If the root of goodness in man be small, in the long-run worldly affairs are like thick weeds choking it.   Although these people should begin worshipping and supporting the Buddhas, they only become the seed to be born in a better state among men or in the abode of the lower gods, or may become the seed of the two lower schools of Buddhism, or may cultivate the great school.   But goodness is uncertain—it may have taken root or may not.   Or if men serve the Buddhas, though they have not served them very long, yet, on account of going through special circumstances, they also may strike root and grow.   This will only be if they regard the Buddhas in a special manner ; or if they also learn from the followers of the two lower schools, they also may grow.   On account of following the example of others, they also may grow.   Those progressing for these latter reasons are all uncertain.   When they meet adverse circumstances, they fall back from the highest Faith to the two lower ones.

b. Next, what is the progress of perfect faith? Briefly speaking, it is threefold. First, it is upright, having right thoughts of the eternal. Second, it is profound, rejoicing to study everything that is good and to practise it. Third, it is greatly pitiful, anxious to deliver all living beings from their sorrow.

QUESTION 8. Formerly you said that all the universe was but one state and that the natures of the gods were not different from that of men, so how is it that it is not only by the study of the Eternal and by practice of all kinds of goodness that one reaches that state?

ANSWER. Man's nature is like a great precious stone. It is bright and pure, but there is the dross of the quarry on it. If men think only of its precious nature, and do not use various means to cleanse it, it will never be pure. Thus is it with mankind. The nature of the eternal in them is absolute purity, but it is defiled with infinite dross. If men only think of the eternal, and do not use various means to improve their nature, they also will never get pure, because there is infinite dross pervading everything. The practice of all sorts of good is in order to purge away the dross. If men practise all sorts of good, they will naturally fall in with the eternal way.

c. Briefly speaking, the means are of four kinds—

(1) Cultivate the root of things, by looking on the true nature of all things as eternal, without beginning, independent of man's conception of things, and not permanent in temporary life; by looking on all things linked together by a never-failing law of deeds and their consequences; by nourishing a great pity and cultivating virtue joyfully; by seeking to save all men, not resting in the nirvana of the two lower schools, as that which does nothing, for the Eternal Archetype never rests.

(2) Cease from evil. It is by contrition and repentance that one is enabled to cease from all evil and prevent its increase. As one follows the Eternal Nature he departs from all evil.

(3) Grow in goodness. It is by diligently honouring and supporting the Three Precious Ones, praising them, rejoicing in their good deeds, and by seeking instructions of the Enlightened. As there is love and respect for the holy character of the Three Precious Ones, faith grows and one desires to get the highest truth.

Besides the influence of God, there is that of His law throughout the universe, and that of the priesthood, the teachers of this law, by which one is able to remove the hindrances to goodness and be firmly rooted in it; for one follows and obeys eternal law and leaves mad hindrances far behind.

(4) Seek the Eternal's wish. It is an ever-growing desire to save all living beings without

exception, so that all may reach the Supreme Nirvana (Rest) of the Higher Faith, where one follows and obeys the nature of the Eternal for ever. The Eternal nature is vast and pervading all living beings without distinction of this, that, or the other, and is the final rest of all.

d. As an intelligent saint (Pusa) thus progresses in religion, he begins to comprehend a little of the Eternal state. As he comprehends the Eternal, he discovers that the Eternal has made eight kinds of sacrifices for men. He descends from his heaven of ease (the Tow Swai). He becomes incarnate and mingles with less fortunate beings. He grows in the womb of obscurity. He becomes well known. He sacrifices all other interests, even his home, and becomes a priest devoted to the Eternal. He knows true religion. He preaches the law of the Eternal. He enters the true nirvana of perfect peace.

But this intelligent saint (Pusa) is not called the divine eternal embodiment. As in the innumerable ages of the past there still remain some deeds which he has not been able to free entirely from defilement, so there are sufferings corresponding to them in his circumstances, but he is not bound by these imperfections any longer.

Since he is free by the power of the Great Eternal to save men, the Sutra says if we speak of the Pusa going down to some evil place he is not really degraded thereby. It is only in the beginning that it appears so, and therefore he descends to strengthen some who are hesitating in fear.

f. Moreover, the saint from the beginning of his perfect faith is far from having any weakness, and never has any fear of falling back to the state of the two lower schools. Even if he hear that nirvana cannot be obtained till after patient toil through troubles lasting for immeasurable and endless kalpas of longest durations, still he faints not, as by faith he knows that behind all existence there is naturally the supreme nirvana (Rest).

2. Growth in intelligent practice. One must know that there must be growth. When the Pusa saints who from the first follow the correct faith are about to complete the first term of long kalpas, they then fully comprehend the Eternal. It is in a state of complete independence of all form, and they practise those five divine exercises (Paramitas) by means of which they pass into the supreme nirvana. (1) As they learn that the Eternal has no selfishness, they then follow obediently the practice of all kinds of divine charity. (2) As they learn that the Eternal is undefiled, free from the sins arising from the longings of the five senses, they obediently practise divine perseverance. (3) As they learn that the Eternal is all-enduring, they obediently practise divine endurance. (4) As they learn that the

Eternal is ever clear, without confusion, they obediently practise divine unchangeableness. (5) As they learn that the Eternal is all intelligence, free from ignorance, they obediently practise divine wisdom or judgments.

3. Growth in attainments. This covers the ground from the beginning of the holy pure state up to the highest attainments of sainthood (Pusaship). What attainments are these? They are those of the Eternal. According to the perception of the senses, this would be called the objective world, but in our present attainment there is nothing outward but the eternal wisdom which is called the Divine Body.

a. These Pusas in an instant are able to reach all space throughout all the universe, adoring all the enlightened gods (Buddhas), and requesting them to explain the Eternal law for the sole purpose of teaching and benefiting all living beings, so as to get the spirit of the law and not mere fine words. These saints sometimes hurry over various stages of progress so as to get right enlightenment speedily in order to help the weak ; sometimes, after a term of countless long kalpas, they may become Buddhas in order to encourage the weary ones, and thus show by countless ways how to attain Buddhaship. In reality, as the root of the nature of the seed of sainthood is the same, the growth is the same and the attainment is the same, namely, through the Eternal way. There is no such thing as omitting any term, as all the saints must go through the three terms, though they follow different ways with different men. As men's nature, desires, and dispositions are different, the saints use different methods for their salvation.

b. Here the growth of this state of sainthood is threefold and is very necessary. The first is that of the true soul, which in no way differs from the Eternal. The second is that of the different means employed to meet the needs of all beings. The third is that of his conceptions of things, where still linger a few false notions disturbing him.

c. Then comes the saint perfection in all virtues at the head of the world of form, showing themselves as the greatest of mortals. In a moment they correspond exactly to the Eternal Wisdom, and all ignorance being entirely gone, this correspondence is called the root seed of all wisdom. These saints naturally possess powers beyond all thought, able to manifest themselves throughout all points of space for the good of all beings.

QUESTION 9. As space is infinite, worlds are infinite. As worlds are infinite, living beings are infinite. As living beings are infinite, the differences of thought in them are infinite, and in such a state their respective magnitudes cannot be determined, none can know or explain them. If ignorance is removed, then no vain guesses will exist. How can we understand that which is called the seed of wisdom ?

ANSWER. All the universe originally was only *One Soul* needing not to conjecture at things. As living beings only imperfectly see the world outside them, their minds are limited and they begin to make idle conjectures different from the reality, thus preventing a right understanding of things. All the Buddhas and Ju Lai (Incarnate Models) are independent of the senses and omniscient. The real soul is the nature of all things. This soul shines forth on all minds. It has great wisdom in innumerable ways, according to the different needs of men so as to instruct them in all kinds of ways. On this account it has been named the seed of all wisdom.

QUESTION 10. If the Buddhas have a natural power to manifest themselves everywhere for the good of all living beings, and if all beings see their manifested bodies, then men observe their various modifications; and if they hear their words, which are good, how do you say that most people cannot see them ?

ANSWER. The divine nature of the Buddhas and of Ju Lai is one pervading all space without any

effort of the mind, therefore we say it is natural,
yet depending on men for its manifestation. The
soul of living beings is just like a mirror. If it is
not clear it cannot reflect. So if the soul of living
beings is not pure, the divine nature cannot be
properly reflected.

CHAPTER IV

The Practice of the Mahayana Faith

Having illustrated the principles, we now discuss
the practice of them. This is on account of those
who have not entered the ranks of the upright ones,
and so we explain the practice of Faith. What
faith? what practice? Briefly speaking, faith is
of four kinds. First, belief in the root of all
things—that is, rejoicing to think of God, the
True Model. Second, belief in the infinite merits
of divinity (Buddhahood), ever thinking of it,
drawing near to it, supporting and adoring it,
growing in goodness, and seeking all wisdom from
it. Third, belief in the great benefit of the Law,
always thinking how to practise all the different
means of salvation. Fourth, belief in the Priesthood's ability to cultivate the right doctrine;
having themselves found good, they help others
to obtain it; ever rejoicing to approach all the

saints, and seeking to learn and practise the truth as it is in the Eternal.

To realise the faith, practice consists of *five stages.* These five are—

1. The stage of charity.
2. The stage of holiness.
3. The stage of enduring wrong.
4. The stage of perseverance.
5. The stage of preventing vain thoughts, and the practice of divine wisdom or judgments.

A. How to practise the state of charity. If one sees any coming to beg in their need, money should be given them according to one's ability in order to prevent covetousness in oneself and to make the poor glad. If one sees men in trouble, fear, and danger, the fear should be relieved according to one's power. If men come to inquire about religion, one should explain the various means according to one's ability. In all things one should not seek the honours of fame or wealth, but, simply feeling that, having received benefit oneself, one should impart the same benefit to others, so that they may return to true wisdom.

B. How to practise the state of holiness. This is to observe the *Ten Commandments—*

1. Thou shalt not kill anything.
2. Thou shalt not steal.
3. Thou shalt not commit adultery

4. Thou shalt not be doublefaced.

5. Thou shalt not curse.

6. Thou shalt not lie.

7. Thou shalt not speak vanity.

8. Thou shalt keep far from coveting.

9. Thou shalt not insult, deceive, flatter, or trick.

10. Thou shalt be free from anger and heresy.

As for the priests, in order to overcome the temptations of the world they should keep far from the stir of the world and ever live in quietness, cultivating few desires and satisfaction with their lot, while mortifications should take place after committing the smallest sin. Their hearts must be moved with fear and most sincere repentance, and in no way must they regard the prohibitions of Ju Lai lightly. They should also guard against appearances of evil, lest men should commit the sin of speaking evil against the priesthood.

C. How to practise the state of bearing the cross (enduring wrong). This is what is called the duty of enduring the aspersions of others without a feeling of revenge through the eight storms of life. That is, to be the same in prosperity, in adversity, in honour and dishonour, in good and evil report, in trouble and in joy.

D. How to practise the state of perseverance. The heart must be never weary in well-doing

8

of all sorts, having a purpose firm and strong, far
from any weakness.   Thinking of having passed in
vain through all the great sorrows of mind and
body down through past ages without doing any
good is sad; to advance in the scale of being
one should diligently practise all sorts of good.
Having obtained good oneself, one should make
this known to others, so as to speedily leave all
sorrow.

Next, although some men practise faith, yet, as
from former generations they had many grave sins
and delusions, they are troubled by all sorts of evil
spirits, or are bound by all sorts of affairs of the
world, or are troubled with sicknesses or with many
other trials; they must therefore have courage
and diligence, and worship God (Buddha) night and
day at all the appointed times, repent with all
sincerity, seek light from Buddha, rejoice with
others' good so as to return towards true wisdom.
This should be done constantly without intermission,
so as to escape from all delusions and to grow in
all goodness.

E. How to practise the state of checking idle
thought and of cultivating sound judgment.   To
check idle thought is to cease from being misled by
impressions and to follow and obey the rules.   To
reflect is to differentiate between the different laws
of temporary existence and to obey the rules of
sound judgment.   How are these to be followed?

These two states are to be gradually cultivated, not independently, but simultaneously.

1. As to the practice of checking vain thoughts, it should be done in a quiet place, properly seated and in a proper spirit. It is not the practice of breathing air in a special manner into the body, as is the custom of some religions, thinking thereby to get the vital spirit of nature into the body, nor the use of anything that has form or colour, whether of empty space or of the four elements earth, water, fire, and wind, or even of the knowledge gained by any experience of the senses, for all kinds of ideas as soon as thought of must be put away, even the idea of banishing them must also be put away. As all existence originally came to be without any idea of its own, it ceases to be also without any idea of its own ; any thoughts arising therefore must be from being absolutely passive. Nor must one follow the mind in its excursions to everything outside itself and then chase that thought away. If the mind wanders far away, it must be brought back into its proper state. One should know that the proper state is that of the soul alone without anything outside of it. Again, even this soul has no form and no thought by which we can conceive of it properly.

a. Having risen from the sitting posture, whether in going out or coming in, or in any work, at all times one should think of the means of checking vain thoughts, and should examine whether he succeeds in it or whether he follows them. In time one gets perfect in the practice and the mind is at rest. As the mind is at rest it gradually gets courage to proceed; in this way it reaches the peace of the Eternal, far beyond all trouble with faith, increasing so that it will soon be so perfect as never to fail any more. But doubters, unbelievers, blasphemers, great sinners, those who are conceited, who will not persevere, and such-like people, cannot obtain this peace of the Eternal.

b. Note next that by this peace one knows that in the spiritual world the peace of the spiritual bodies of all the Buddhas and of all living bodies are one and the same, and is called divine peace. Know that the root of this peace is in the Eternal. If this is continued, there gradually arises in the mind an infinite peace.

c. If there should be some men without the strength which comes from good deeds who are troubled with evil spirits and the gods and demons of outside religions, appearing sometimes in ugly forms, causing fear to them whilst sitting in contemplation, at other times appearing in lovely forms to tempt them, they should think of the *One Eternal Soul*, then these appearances will vanish and give no more trouble. These evil spirits, whether taking the form of the heavenly beings, of Pusa saints, or of Ju Lai, all full of perfection, or using magic formulæ, or preaching charity, morality, endurance of wrong, perseverance, contemplation, wisdom, or discussing the one unseen reality, the formless reality, the passionless reality, without enmity and without love, without cause and without effect—nothing but pure emptiness—say that this is the true nirvana! They also teach men how to know the past and to know the future, and how to know what is in the mind of others, and how to have unfailing gifts of speech, causing men to covet the fame and wealth of this world.

Or, again, these evil spirits cause men to be frequently violently angry or very happy, without anything to steady them; sometimes to have great compassion, or to be sleepy or ill, or to be without perseverance; or they cause men to persevere for a time and then to fall back worse than ever, to lose faith, to have many doubts and fears, or give up their practice of checking vain thoughts and make them follow miscellaneous matters and be chained by the many affairs of the world, so as to give men a certain kind of peace, somewhat similar to the true peace, but which is the product of outside religions and not the true peace of the Eternal.

Or, again, these evil spirits cause men for one, two, three, or even seven days, to remain in contemplation, as if enjoying delicious food; they are most happy in mind and body without any hunger or thirst; or they may be led to eat without any control, sometimes much and sometimes little, so that the countenance changes, and exhibits gladness or sorrow accordingly.

As there are such things, religious people should always wisely examine themselves, lest their minds should fall into the nets of heresy. They should carefully rectify their thoughts, and neither adopt nor be attached to them, but keep themselves far from all delusions.

One should know that the peace of outside religions is of the senses, of the affections, to gratify self, desiring the honours of fame and the wealth of the world.

But the true peace is not in the realms of the senses or in possessions, and even after contemplation there is neither the feeling of having attained perfection with no further effort, nor conceit for what has been accomplished. All trials gradually diminish.

If men do not cultivate this peace, there is no other way to get the seed of Ju Lai, the Incarnate Lord.

As the peace of this world mostly arises from the pleasure which is given to the senses, it is bound to the three worlds of form, of desire, and of no-form, like that of the outside religions. Once men leave the guidance of sound wisdom, there arise at once false doctrines.

d. Next note that those who diligently set their

minds on securing this peace should in the present generation obtain ten advantages—

(1) All the Buddhas and Pusa saints throughout all space always protect them.

(2) None of the evil spirits can cause them any fear.

(3) They cannot be deceived by any of the ninety-five kinds of outside religions.

(4) They are far beyond questioning the deep things of the Buddhist religion, and great sins gradually diminish.

(5) There is an end to all doubt and all kinds of heresies.

(6) Faith in the world of Ju Lai (God Incarnate) grows.

(7) They leave sorrow far behind in the minds of mortals, while they themselves have no fear.

(8) Their spirits become gentle and peaceable, they put off pride and conceit, and are not troubled by other people's opinions.

(9) Although they have not obtained full peace at all times and in every place, they are able to lessen their trials, and do not covet the world's pleasures.

(10) When their peace is secured, they are unmoved by any seductions of outside attractions.

2. Now, if men practise only contemplation, the mind is damped, or gets weary, and does

not rejoice in all goodness, but is far from pity, therefore it is necessary to cultivate reasoning or reflection.

a. One should reflect that nothing made throughout the universe can last long; in a moment it may be destroyed.

b. One should reflect that all thought rises and vanishes again like a wave, and is therefore a sorrow.

c. One should reflect that all the past is misty like a dream, that all the present is like lightning, that all the future rises suddenly like a cloud in the sky.

d. One should reflect that the bodies of all living beings are unclean, full of all kinds of uncleanness, and therefore not to be rejoiced in.

e. Thus one should reflect that all living beings, from eternity down the ages, being influenced by ignorance, live and die and endure all the great sorrows of mind and body; and reflect on the endless trials of the present and on the immeasurable sorrows of the future, which cannot be got rid of and which men are scarcely aware of. When all men's lives are so full of sorrow, they are greatly to be pitied.

f. Having thought of these things, one should stir oneself up to make a GREAT VOW to lead one's own soul to leave the finite and gain the infinite, cultivate every means of grace to deliver all men for ever from their sorrows and obtain the highest joys of nirvana.

g. Having made this great vow, one must not give up practising it or be weary in it, but at all times and all places engage in every good that is in one's power.

3. Whilst sitting in meditation, one's mind should be bent on checking vain thoughts. At other times one should reflect carefully in regard to everything whether it should or should not be done. Whether walking or resting, lying down or rising up, both reflecting and checking vain thoughts should go together. This is what is meant by the saying that although we practise all these things, our perfection is not really produced by ourselves, but by the nature of the Eternal working through us.

Again, thinking of the never-failing law of cause and effect, and joy and sorrow as the reward of good and evil, when we think of law we must also think of this goal so difficult to attain.

The practice of checking vain thoughts is to sever the attachments of ordinary men to the world, and to put away the fears and weaknesses of the two lower schools of Buddhism.

The practice of reflection is to deliver from the narrow sin of the two lower schools, who do not have the vow of great pity for others, and who do not keep far from ordinary men who do not practise goodness.

In this way the two methods of reflection and vain thoughts are mutually helpful to one another and inseparable. If both are not practised, one cannot then enter on the way of wisdom.

4. Next consider those who begin to learn the five methods of this chapter, p. 107, and desire to get right faith, but are timid and weak. As they live in this world of extreme suffering, they fear they cannot constantly approach God (Buddha) and personally contribute to His service. Thus they fear they cannot attain to this perfect faith, and have a mind to renounce their search after it.

These should know that Ju Lai has most excellent means to strengthen their faith. It is by having the mind set only on the things of God (Buddha), and by desiring that one may be born in another world of Buddha and be constantly with Him for ever, far from all evil, that one may attain this end. As the Sutra says, if a man sets his mind to think only of God (Amitabha Buddha), who is in the happiest realm of the west (Paradise), and if his good deeds are in the right direction, and if he desires to get to that happy Paradise, he will then get there; and as he is always in the presence of Buddha, he will never fall back.

If we reflect on the eternal nature of God

(Amitabha Buddha), and constantly practise this method, one will in the end reach the place of true wisdom.

CHAPTER V

THE ADVANTAGES OF THE PRACTICE OF
THE MAHAYANA FAITH

Having discussed the practice of these principles we will now discuss the advantages of practising them. We have already given a general idea of the mysterious resources of the Buddhas of the Mahayana school.

A. If any one desires to get a right faith in the deep things of Ju Lai, and desires to be far from error, which brings religion into disrepute, and to get the Mahayana Faith, he should lay hold of this book, study it and practise it. In the end he will attain to the very highest truth.

B. If a man listens to this truth, and has neither fear nor weakness, such a man is certain to succeed to the rank of Buddha, and to be enrolled as such by all the Divine Ones.

C. If a man should be able to reform all living beings throughout all the systems in the universe, in order to make them good, he would not be equal to a man who for only the time he takes to a meal studies this way of deliverance. The two methods are incomparable.

D. Next, if a man takes this book, studies and practises it only for a day and a night, the blessings received would be incalculable. Even if all the Buddhas of the universe were each to speak of these blessings for incalculably and immeasurably long kalpas, they could not exhaust them, for the blessings of the Eternal Nature are endless, and the blessings to this man would be also in like manner endless.

E. But if there should be any who speak evil and do not believe in this book, the recompense of their sin will be to suffer immense pain for measureless ages. On this account all men should respectfully believe and not speak evil of it, thereby injuring themselves more and more and others too, destroying every hope of deliverance by destroying the Eternal Soul of the Three Precious Ones originally in man (the soul of the universe, the body of laws pervading the universe, the body of men teaching these laws), for all the Divine Ones attain to nirvana by this means, and all the Saints attain Buddha-wisdom by the same practice.

F. Know that it is by this means that the Pusa saints of the past obtained pure faith, and that it is by this means that the Pusa saints of the present obtain pure faith, therefore it is by this means that the Pusa saints of the future must

obtain pure faith.   Thus all men should diligently
study and practise it.

THE CLOSING HYMN

Deep and wide is Buddhist Law,
This in brief I have declared ;
Godward are eternal stores,
Blessings give to countless worlds !

IV

TRANSLATOR'S INTRODUCTION TO
THE LOTUS SCRIPTURE

Miao Fa Lien Hua King

(Nanjio's *Catalogue of Tripitaka*, No. 134)

1. *Its Importance.*

Its importance is apparent when we find that
it is the most popular of all Buddhist Scriptures
in Japan. Though Buddhism there has twelve
different sects, yet I found the Lotus Scripture on
the lecterns of every Buddhist temple visited. It
is also the chief Scripture in the Tiendai school
of Buddhism in China, and is therefore the chief
source of consolation to the many millions of
Buddhists in the Far East.

Its importance is also manifest when we
discover that its chief teaching of Life, Light, and
Love is in the main the same as that found in
the Gospel of St. John, the consolation of all the
devout in Christendom. The Lotus Scripture is

nearly the same size as the four Gospels and Acts put together.

2. *History of the Text.*

It existed before A.D. 250, according to the *Sacred Books of the East,* vol. xxi. p. 22. But where it came from we do not yet know. Some suspect it has an Egyptian origin.

There are three principal translations of it made from Sanscrit into Chinese, namely—

By Dharmerakcha between A.D. 265 and 316, in twenty-eight chapters.

By Kumaragiva between A.D. 384 and 417, in twenty-eight chapters.

By Gnanagupta and Dharmagupta between A.D. 589 and 618, in twenty-seven chapters.

The last purposes to contain additions to supply the incompleteness of the first two versions. These are numbered 138, 134, 139 respectively in Nanjio's *Catalogue.*

Burnouf first translated it into French, and Kern translated it into English, *S.B.E.,* vol. xxi.

3. *Why translate it again?*

When this natural question is asked, the answer is easy, though long, in order to make it clear.

First, it is most important to bear in mind that a large class of Buddhist Scripture, called the Fang

Têng Scriptures, in Sanscrit Vaipulia, were amplified and diffuse editions of later date than the originals. These were first introduced into China by Dharmaraksha in A.D. 266–317 (Eitel). The immense amount of utterly incredible local Indian colouring, as seen in Kern's translation, makes one long for the essence which is the manna on which so many millions feed.

This we now find in an edition translated into Japanese by K. S. Fukagawa and published by the Buddhist Nichiren sect in A.D. 1904, in ten volumes. Eight of which contain the Lotus Gospel (I call it Gospel because of its wonderful similarity to the Christian Gospels), and two other volumes are what might be called the Prologue and Epilogue to it respectively.

Besides the Japanese text, there is in it, in parallel columns, on the top of the page, a Chinese synopsis of the Scripture which leaves out the incredible Indian embellishments, giving only the essence of the teaching. This synopsis is not new by a Chinaman or a Japanese, but consists of extracts made from the original Chinese translation of Kumaragiva, so as to give the essence of this Scripture with its Prologue and Epilogue.

This synopsis or essence is what I now translate. It has never been translated into any European language before.

9

4. *Order of Chapters.*

The order of the chapters in the Lotus Gospel
is not the same in the Japanese version from which
I have translated as that of Kern, which is from
a Sanscrit version.   I received my copy from the
chief abbot of the Nichiren sect of Buddhism at
Ikegani Tokyo.   The order in each is as follows :—

Kern.	Japanese.
I–X	I–X are in the same order.
XI	XI–XII
XII–XXIV	XIII–XXV
XXV	XXVII
XXVI ?	XXVIII
XXVII ?	XXVI

The Nichiren sect of Buddhism makes the
Lotus Gospel its main one, but has added two other
Buddhist Scriptures to it—one as a Prologue on
Boundless Righteousness or Eternal Life, and the
other, as an Epilogue on Pu Hien Pusa, or Saint of
Universal Good.

5. *Apostolic and Patristic Apologetics.*

The attitude of the primitive missionaries of
the patristic period in China towards Buddhism is
full of valuable instruction to modern missionaries,
as it reveals the *secret* of their success in con-
ciliating and winning over the early Buddhists,
not only to tolerate, but also to teach the higher

doctrines of Christianity. For example, the following verse is found printed at the head of several of the most popular Mahayana Sutras—

> Highest, deepest Law profound
> Saves from sorrows, countless woes,
> Now I study to discover
> The true meaning of Jü Lai.

Here we have an example of the Ancient Mystery teachings of Religion. They were not revealed to the multitude. Even our Lord spoke only in parables, allegories—"dark sayings"—to the multitudes. It was only to the disciples, His initiated, that He spoke clearly (St. John xvi. 29, R.V.).

It is well also to bear in mind our Lord's attitude to other religions. He did not come to destroy, but to fulfil. St. Paul quoted Greek poets with approval in his sermon at Athens. Justin Martyr and St. Augustine referred to other religions as being also derived from God, only that Christianity was fuller and more perfect. This, too, is the teaching of the latest and best authorities on comparative religion in our days.

The remarkable Sakyamuni prophesy, of a higher Teacher of religion than himself well illustrates this, much like the Jewish prophecies of the coming Messiah. Sakyamuni in the sixth chapter of the Diamond Sutra, said—

"Five hundred years after my death, there will

rise another Teacher of religion who will produce faith by the fulfilment of this prophecy. You should know that He will plant the root of His teaching, not in one, two, three, four or five Buddhas, nor in ten thousand Buddhas, but plant it at the root of all the Buddhas; when that One comes, according to this prophecy, then have faith in Him at once, and you will obtain incalculable blessings."

6. *Modern Apologetics.*

Once the truer Copernican system of the Universe had superseded the Ptolemaic, fresh ideas sprang up, giving to us new continents—America, Africa, and Australasia.

When men thoroughly studied the value of steam and electricity they became godlike in power, and created a new heaven and a new earth, or rather reduced their dimensions, so that messages which a century ago would take years to transmit, can now be sent in a few minutes.

Turning to the spiritual world, the result of new ideas is not less startling. The conception of powerful tribal and national gods which encouraged men to make warlike aggressions for selfish ends, has given way to the conception of one Universal Ruler of heaven and earth, and to the brotherhood of all nations, and it should, therefore, make men cease from war and love and help each other.

From this view we are beginning to reap important results in arbitration—treaties, and the progress of Peace principles generally, and the Hague Conference.

The conception that God had chosen a particular race or caste, to be the sole depository of His Truth, and the sole spiritual guide of mankind, is now known to all leaders of thought to be an exploded theory.

Our Lord Jesus Christ is " the Light of *every one* that cometh into the world." St. Paul was specially to be the Apostle to the Gentiles, so that they also, as well as the Jews, might become spiritual teachers.

Since God is the great Father of all, and " so loved the world that He gave His only begotten Son " to save it, it is incredible that He should leave all outside the Jews and Christians without any knowledge of the *Way of Salvation.*

Modern research has now made it abundantly clear, that before the Jewish nation existed, *God* had given true and right ideas to some in Babylonia, Egypt, and in the land of Midian, which greatly influenced both Abraham and Moses.

Nor were these the only channels through which spiritual truth was transmitted. The New Testament, in the clearest possible language, says that

" In *every* nation he that feareth God, and worketh righteousness, is accepted of Him."

In China we possess the lofty Ethics of Confucius, advocating Benevolence, Righteousness, Propriety, Knowledge, and Mutual Confidence, in as strong and eloquent language as that of any of the Hebrew prophets. With regard to the doctrine of Immortality taught in the New Testament to Western nations—we find that in the Far East, there is what might be called a Fifth Gospel, or "the Lotus Gospel," which for fifteen centuries has shone throughout the Buddhist world in China, Korea, and Japan with such brilliancy, that countless millions trust to its light alone, for their hope of Immortal Life. It will be abundantly evident to Western students, that the wonderful truths taught therein have precisely the same ring as those taught in the Fourth Gospel, about the *Life*, the *Light*, and the *Love*. The bearing of the Cross, by patient endurance of wrong and undeserved insults, is also inculcated over and over again, in the same gentle language as that of the Apostle of Love himself.

7. *The value of Comparative Religion.*

The reader may possibly ask—If this be so, what further need is there of sending missionaries from the West, to China and Japan, when they possess this priceless treasure?" I reply: For two reasons—

First, because modern Christianity is the winnowing fan, which separates the chaff from the wheat;

secondly, because Christianity helps to replace atheism by faith in God.

Countless " Buddhas," vague " worlds," endless mythologies, require to be well sifted in order to separate the golden grains of wheat from the worthless chaff. The doctrines of New Buddhism (the Mahayana school) now taught, are so intermingled and mixed up with Old Buddhism, and transmigration concepts (derived from ancient Indian thought), that only those who possess the fuller light of Christianity can recognise in them the likeness to true Christianity.

For example, the story of Kwanyin, given in the 25th chapter of the Lotus Gospel, is an Eastern allegory, of the Infinite Love and Compassion of God. It matters little whether " Kwanyin " as an individual ever existed. The important point is that Infinite Love and Compassion is raised to an ideal, that inspires the life of all good men and women just as in the parable of the Prodigal Son in our Third Gospel we Christians have the ideal of Infinite Tenderness and Forgiveness presented to us as a model of what God the Father is.

It is worth noting that Chinese Buddhism is now degenerate, and that comparatively few attend the services, due to the fact that the priests are not drawn from the higher intellectual ranks of society, but too often from the lowest, and are not educated like the Confucianists.

Some years ago I stayed for weeks in a Buddhist monastery, and took my meals with the Buddhist Abbot, who was there for the special purpose of training and ordaining new priests. A course of fifty odd days was considered sufficient to fit them for ordination! This is the case even now, when I witnessed two hundred and eighty new priests being ordained in Peking in 1910. How can such men lead Confucianists who have spent twenty years in diligent study? The best Buddhist teachers in China are found amongst educated Confucianists who were converted to Buddhism after completing their Confucian education.

But I have been present at Buddhist services, in various parts of Japan, where the reverence and devotion are unsurpassed by Christian worshippers.

One August morning, I witnessed one of the daily services held at sunrise in Kyoto, at which over five hundred worshippers were present, more than half of them were men before going to business. Such a sight I have never seen anywhere in Christendom.

Besides this it has been a joy to me to find many Japanese priests studying Comparative Religion, and consequently our Christian Scriptures, with a zeal and intelligence which Christian teachers might well emulate, for without thorough knowledge of the religion of others there cannot be intelligent sympathetic teaching of our own.

I am told on good authority, that most measures for the public good in Japan are led by those professing the Buddhist Faith. The extraordinary progress made by Japan during the last fifty years, may be attributed to the open-mindedness of her people, their willingness and anxiety to learn the " *best* " of everything as inculcated in Confucianism and in this Lotus Gospel, both of which the Japanese have adopted. In this particular, the Japanese have proved themselves to be faithful followers of the " Gleam," and so have reaped the promised reward. It is only fair to recognise these noble traits in the character of the devout in the Farthest East.

Our Lord promised that the Holy Spirit should guide His disciples into " all truth."

Alas that many blind teachers in the West are teaching that only conventional religious truth is sacred and Divine, the rest is secular and human ! This view of truth has been a great drag on human progress, introducing a vicious conflict with Science, and emptying the churches of intelligent men. Happily there are now many bright prophets as true as those of old. When the leaders of the West and the leaders of the East understand each other better, there will be mutual advantage, and mutual sympathy and help in all that is best. Considering the view so prevalent in the West, that Buddhist salvation is based upon the doctrine of

Karma, it is important to call attention to the repeated assertions in these Scriptures, namely—

1. That of "Boundless Righteousness or Ever-lasting Life" which forms the Introduction or Prologue to the Lotus Gospel.
2. The Lotus Gospel of Life, Light, and Love which is the main Scripture, teaches that there is something far superior to Karma.
3. That of the Boddhisatva, or saint, Pu Hien standing for good-will to men, which is the Lotus conclusion or Epilogue.
4. All these Scriptures declare, again and again, that man is not saved by his own good works alone, but chiefly by the Grace of God.

Hence all the temples abound with votive offer-ings, in gratitude to God for innumerable answered prayers.   All these facts have to be accounted for.

This Faith-Gospel, found in the Far East, teaches that three things are sacred, namely—God, His Laws, and the Teachers of these Laws.   This is neither Greek, Anglican, nor Roman Catholicism (see chapter xix.), but the Catholicity of the Universal Church of God, of pure New Buddhism as well as pure Christianity, to which men and women of this twentieth century are called to return.

When the devotion of the East and West is united, then the kingdoms of this world will soon become the kingdom of our God and of His Christ.

Secondly, missionaries from the West are still needed in the Far East.

Because Christ the Incarnate God replaced the atheism of early Buddhism by faith in God. He is therefore not only the Great Atonement to bring men to God, but is also the Great AT-ONE-MENT, to reconcile the East and West, and bring them into tune. It is at His behest that multitudes of missionaries go forth to all continents and races to-day.

He is described in the New Buddhism of China and Japan, as "the Great Mighty One" *par excellence*, who has broken the chain of Karma and Transmigration, whereby countless millions were bound for unnumbered ages, and has given deliverance by the promise of an immediate entrance into Paradise : "To-day thou shalt be with Me in Paradise." And this, because His incarnation is declared in the Lotus Gospel, to be different in kind from that of all Buddhas.

The words which describe this tremendous change are as follow :—

"Ta shih chih (Jap. Daiseishi) the Great Mighty One 'is' able to save those who being still in the evil path of transmigration could not cross over nor break away from the ocean of ever-recurring rebirths (life and death). Those who see Him can have all their sins committed during limitless kalpas, removed. He is never reborn by the usual process into this lower world. He invariably resides in some of the Buddha lands (mansions of heaven). He always preaches the Law and the Doctrine to great multitudes, and thus acts as the helper of God (Amida Buddha)" (Atkinson's *Prince Siddartha*, p. 259). (See also General Introduction on Buddhist Trinity, p. 12.)

In the Buddhist temple, where the Amitabha Trinity is represented, it is very significant to note that—

1. The central Figure always is Amitabha (Jap. Amida), the Eternal, Ancient of days.

2. On his right hand always is Ta shih chih (Jap. Daiseishi), who has broken the power of sin and death.

3. On Amitabha's left hand always is Kwanyin, the Holy One who hears the prayers of the world.

It is impossible to identify with absolute certainty some of the personified virtues in the Pantheon of the Far East, with the historical religious leaders and saints of the West. But that is not the most important thing.

With the exception of Sakyamuni (called by the Japanese Shaka), who is used in the Buddhist

Scriptures more as God than as an historical character, the names of Kwanyin, Pu Hien, are not historical, but allegorical, like those ladies Beatrice and Lucia in the *Divine Comedy* who led Dante up from the Inferno, through Purgatory into Paradise; and, like "Christian, Evangelist, Hopeful, and Great-heart," in the *Pilgrim's Progress*, portray certain characteristics such as Wisdom, Mercy, Patient endurance of wrong, Divine strength, Spiritual power, etc. etc., and are just as real as the characters in many modern novels drawn from life. Kern also says in his notes to his translation, "In all periods of the creed the Buddha Sakyamuni is only anthropomorphic."

If we find the Far East idealising the same virtues, and condemning the same vices, as we do in the West, is it not a great common working basis for the upbuilding of character from both the Divine and human side, and also the strongest bond of union between East and West?

Surely this should remove a great stumbling-stone, and the varying forms of worship might easily be tolerated just as we suffer differences in national costume and language in local dialects and customs, provided the fundamentals are one and the same.

The most vital point to be noted now is

THE DISCOVERY

that the *same* religious ideals prevail among many, both in the East and in the West, and that they are set forth in these Scriptures for men to materialise in their own lives.

Nor is this all. There are two other most important objects to be gained by this translation—

First, the Unity of all religion. There was a time when every religion considered itself true, and every other false, but that has long been superseded by a more just classification of all the great religions, into good, better, and best. And now we have a further advance by the latest authorities, who say that as there are no longer two sciences of mathematics, or astronomy, or chemistry, or of electricity in the world, the time is now come, to say, that there shall be only *One religion* in the future, and that one will contain what is truest and best in all past religions which reveal the Divine in them.

The second object is to strengthen the forces struggling against the selfish materialism of this age by the united efforts for the promotion of universal good-will, by all the children of God of every race. When the ancient empires of Egypt, Babylon, Persia, Greece, and Rome arose and carried all before them by the might of innumerable legions, which took possession of all lands and

property for their own, religious bodies arose in
Palestine, India, Europe, and Africa, whose aim
was to supersede such iniquity, by adopting the
very opposite methods for universal good.   They
had no army, only preachers of the new kingdom ;
no weapons, but those of knowledge and love.
They renounced all property and family ties,
devoting themselves entirely to study and good-
will to all in quiet monasteries apart from the
turmoil of life.   The object of the one was to take
all, and of the other to give all.   This was the
Great Renunciation of all ascetics, whether Christian or non-Christian.

Many Buddhists and Christians having tried
this method for two thousand years, without gaining
the assent of the leading nations of the earth,
have come to the conclusion that something more
is wanting now, as the materialists become more
materialistic than ever.

8. *Present need—Organised co-operation.*

It is not enough to have profound knowledge
and infinite love, it is also necessary to have power
to enforce international reciprocity and righteousness between classes, without monopolies to any.
We need a great Judge to be the terror of selfish
Governments.   One federated central Government
armed for the whole earth, to enforce the righteous
will of God, instead of a score all armed for their

own ends, is the one great thing lacking now.
And this, the prophets of Righteousness in all
religions have always proclaimed to be one of
the great characteristics of the kingdom of God
on earth.

Now let the clarion call go forth, from all
religions to co-operate in securing this end at once,
without delay.   It is one of the greatest of all
needs, and when attained it will be the greatest
of all blessings, carrying in its train incalculable
other blessings.   When the disciples of the Eastern
and Western Gospel co-operate with each other,
and with others, who are longing and groaning for
the advent of Righteousness, then the great chasm
between nations and races and classes will be
bridged over.   Religion will be crowned with victory
over brute force, and universal peace and blessing
will prevail.

The Eastern religions are mines of gold from
which incalculable stores of great value still lie
hidden in their vast and hoary literature unknown
to the Western mind.   I have only picked up a
few nuggets which the best people of Far Eastern
Asia consider more precious than rubies and which
delight every truth-loving soul of the West, and
most of all those messengers of God who seek to
establish His kingdom in all the earth, based on the
common highest truths inspired of God in all lands
and throughout all the ages, pointing all to strive

for the highest that has been discovered or revealed to man.

With these Introductory remarks I send this book forth, in the hope that it may bring home yet another aspect of the Faith as held by countless millions in the Far East to the dwellers in the Far West.

I shall be grateful to receive any criticisms or emendations from either Chinese, Japanese, or Western students, who are conversant with this beautiful Gospel of " *The White Lotus.*"

V

THE ESSENCE OF THE LOTUS SCRIPTURE: PROLOGUE

THE SCRIPTURE OF ETERNAL LIFE

[The Text of this Essence is selected by a Chinese Buddhist from passages in the Wu Liang I King Naujio's Catalogue, No. 133. Trans.]

CHAPTER I

Its Character.

The Gate of Infinite Law [1]
Explains all things,
Opens the Way to the Immortal,[2]

[NOTE ABOUT THE REFERENCES. For most of these numerous references and footnotes I am indebted to the unwearied services of the Hon. Mrs. E. A. Gordon, who has studied Buddhism and Shintoism in Japan so sympathetically and thoroughly, that some of the leading priests there say that she knows their religion better than any foreigner in their land.—T. R.]

[1] "Truly great and wonderful is their Teaching, O King, to him that is willing to examine and understand it. . . . Truly blessed is the race of Christians . . . their Teaching is the Gateway of Light."—*Apology of the Philosopher Aristides to the Emperor Hadrian, cir.* A.D. 124–30. See p. 20, note 4.

[2] Cf. p. 156, note 4 ; p. 157, notes 2, 4 ; p. 162, note 1 ; p. 182. The Secret of the Lotus is Immortality.

147

Delivers from the bondage of Custom,[1]
Removes the worries of existence,
And gives great rest to the Soul.
It is a doctrine True and Good,
A great Realm of Bliss
From an unsought Teacher.[2]
It gives a place of calm Joy,
Of Salvation, Protection,
And is a great Defence.[3]
It has a great and faithful Leader,[4]
Who is Eyes for the blind multitude,[5]
A Pilot, the great Pilot ;
A chief Physician,
The great, chief Physician,[6]
A Comforter—
The great Comforter.
Great is this awakening Light !
The great and Holy Lord,
By the incense of His virtue,
Makes all things fragrant.
He has no body to handle,
Nor is He non-existent—
Bodiless.[7]

---

[1] Matt. xv. 2.   See p. 175, note 2.
[2] John xvi.   [3] Isa. xviii. 19.
[4] "Faithful Leader," cf. Isa. lv. 4 ; Rev. i. 5.   Also Heb.
ii. 10, where "Author of Salvation" is rendered also "Captain,"
and is "Prince" in Acts iii. 15, v. 21, "the Prince of Life," *i.e.*
Messiah.   It is the same as "Leader," and may be compared with
Josh. v. 16.
[5] John ix. 39.   [6] Mark i. 2, 3.   [7] John xiv.

The principles of all Goodness
  Come from Him.[1]
Because of this Light
  Pride and insolence disappear.
One becomes a new being.[2]
The heavenly anthem thunders,
With all kinds of music [3] earth resounds,
For this new Life one renounces
Every hindrance,
Wealth, wife, children, city life [4]
Ungrudgingly : in word or thought,
Ready to give head and brains
  For others' weal :
Fearing not sword nor spear,
Nor wounds of curse, nor insult—
  Enjoys a royal calm.[5]

---

[1] John i. 7–10.

[2] "The Wondrous Being, without form or substance, and yet not a Non-Being, for to Him all things owe their existence."—Wang Pi commentator of Lao-tze.

[3] Jas. i. 17.

[4] "A new people and a new race—men that know God, and receive from Him what they ask."—*Apology of Aristides, cir.* A.D. 124–30.   Cf. John iii. 7 ; Gal. ii. 15 ; Eph. ii. 10 ; 2 Cor. v. 17, mg. R.V. "a new Creation."

[5] *The Nihongi* (vol. i. p. 68) recounts that six months after the reception of the Sutras and the Images of the Three Precious Ones from Korea, *i.e.* in the summer of A.D. 553, the following report was received from the province Kahachi : "From within the sea at China, in the province of Idzumi, there is heard a voice of Buddhist chants, which re-echoes like the sound of thunder, a Glory shines like the radiance of the Sun." In his heart the Emperor wondered at this.   Cf. Luke ii. 9–14, xv. 7 ; Rev. viii. 3–5.

Following It one can surmount
All difficulties.

CHAPTER II

Its Teaching

Know well that now whate'er you ask
The Godlike One will quickly grant,[1]
Besides—a hold upon Eternal Life.[2]
After receiving this new Life
You can persuade others
    To forsake their doubts.
There is a Way which enables
    Its students to attain the Highest Wisdom.[3]
This Way is called
    " Eternal Righteousness,"
From Eternity until now
    Its nature is calm.[4]
If evil thoughts arise, causing all kinds of ill,
And transmigration throughout many grades
    Of animal existence,
Suffering all kinds of misery and poison,
Since desires are boundless,
The Remedy must be also boundless ;
Since Law is boundless,

---

[1] John xiv. 13, xv. 8.   [2] John xvii. 3.   [3] Luke i. 76.
[4] " How calm it is, how quiet ! " as Lao-tze said of the Tao.

Righteousness is also boundless.[1]
The Mercy manifested,
Mark well, is real.
The Doctrine of " Eternal Righteousness "
   Is true and upright,
   Honours the Highest.[2]
All the Illumined [3] past, present, and to come,
   Proclaim it.[4]
It uproots the sorrows of all beings,
Is truly great in mercy.
Formerly, when at college,
I studied at the Sages' feet
For six full years—earnestly
Learning their highest wisdom.

---

[1] Rom. v. 18.

[2] Luke ii. 14.

[3] Heb. i. 1. "Illumined," another term derived from the Mysteries; compare "Enlightened" in Heb. vi. 4, x. 32, R.V.; also 2 Cor. iv. 11–16. φοτισμος, "illuminated," was the title given to the Christian neophytes in the first centuries. See p. 175, note 1; p. 192, note 1.

[4] See p. 153, note 2; p. 202, note 1; p. 219, note 5. The Indian Sakyamuni always maintained that the Religion revealed to him was the Age then present; and that the Buddhas who had preceded him in the immeasurable ages behind all taught the same Truth, namely, "The Way of the Buddhas." Cf. 2 Pet. ii. 5, mg. R.V. "Noah, a Herald of Righteousness"; Jonah iii. 1–5; so also St. Paul was "appointed a Herald and an Apostle" . . . "the Message, i.e. Proclamation, wherewith I was entrusted" (1 Tim. ii. 7, mg. R.V.; Tit. i. 3; 2 Tim. iv. 17, R.V.). It was the arrival of the "Time of Reformation" which was thus proclaimed, the cessation of the "Times of Ignorance"; and "the Way of God" was then explained "more accurately" to those who already knew and followed it. Consult Heb. ix. 10; Acts xvii. 28, xviii. 26; Rev. xiv. 6, R.V.; 1 John ii. 7; Luke iii. 2–4.

I learned that men's dispositions
And desires differ ;
And that among them
Are all varieties of doctrine taught,
Whose one aim is to produce Good works.
But though, for forty years,
I practised them,
I failed to grasp the highest Truth—
Therefore I with others turned to seek religion
In some different way,[1]
Having failed to reach
    The Highest Wisdom, I saw [2]
In the river, in the stream,
In the well and in the lake,
In the brook and in the ditch,
And in the vast ocean,
The nature of the water is the same,
Although, apparently, it differs.
The beginning, middle, ending
Of men's speech may differ,
The phrasing follows one grammatic rule,
    Giving one meaning.
So, in Religion, first we teach

---

[1] Cf. Gal. i. 6, 7, R.V. "called in the grace of Christ unto a
different gospel ; which is not another gospel." Also p. 169,
note 1 ; on the differences between Hinayana the Old and
Mahayana the New Buddhism, none of whose sacred writings, Sutras,
are of earlier date than the second half of the first century A.D.
Acts iv. 12 ; 1 Cor. i. 21-24, ii. 6-10.

[2] Gen. i. 31.

"The four Degrees of Saintship,"
   In the Hinayana School.
To win the chief degree
   The Middle School awards,
We teach "the Twelve Causes and Effects."
In the advanced Mahâyâna School
We teach "the Twelve Fang Têng [1] Books."
All the Buddhas—the Illumined Ones—
Teach the same secret,
   From age to age,
That their Goal is God ! [2]
Should you desire soon to attain
   The Highest Wisdom,
You must learn and practise
The profound and highest Doctrine—
The Scripture of "Eternal Righteousness," [3]
The Buddhism of the Mahâyâna School.

Chapter III

Its Effects

   After untold kalpas of sorrow
   Men fail to reach the Highest Wisdom,
   Because they do not know

---

[1] See note to Introduction, p. 131 ; also p. 255, note 5.

[2] Professor F. Delitzsch says that the signification of the Hebrew word for God—El—is Goal. See p. 150, note 3.

[3] Matt. xvi. 26.

How straight the Right Way is,[1]
Therefore they take the wrong,
And fall into many snares.
This Scripture originally came
From the home of all Illumined Saints [2]
To sow the Seed of Wisdom
In the hearts of all mankind,
And abide wherever its disciples are.
Its effects are absolutely
  Immeasurable.
It makes those who once were
Without aim in life [3]
Desire to save their fellow-men.
  With one turn,
  With one hymn,
  With one phrase,
There opens up before them
A boundless vista of Righteousness,
Reaching beyond this mortal life.
Quite fearlessly,
Like their Guide, they pass
  From death to Life : [4]

[1] "The Great Tao is very level and easy, but men loved the by-ways."—Lao-tze, B.C. 550.

[2] Cf. Acts iii. 24, R.V. ; Luke xxiv. 25–27 ; Acts xvii. 2–4. See p. 4, note 3.

[3] 2 Cor. v. 9–10, R.V. : " We make it our aim—our ambition, mg. to be well pleasing unto Him."

[4] See p. 148, note 4.   Fu, who is worshipped in China with the invocation " Omi to Fu " (the Chinese equivalent of the Japanese " Namu Amida Butsu "), is called "the Guiding Buddha " Tsie-

Like Him they pass
  From death to Life.
Although they have not crossed themselves
They are able to aid others crossing over.
  A youthful princely heir,
Although unable to manage State affairs,
Becomes at once revered by Ministers of State.
King and queen, with love abounding,
Constantly speak of him.
  Wherefore ?
Because he is young and helpless.
The King of all Illumined Ones
United to this Lotus Bride,
Together they give birth to many Saints.
Already, in all spheres, they have from every
    class
Won deep respect.
Such, evermore receiving help
From all the Buddhas—the Illumined Ones,[1]
Their love abounds to overflowing
Because of this new Law,
Though still beset with trouble
(Not having left all earthly cares behind),
Still can they show the Bodhisatvas' Way.
Like the great Dragon

yin-Fu, for He guides the disciple to Paradise. John v. 24, R.V.,
John viii. 51 ; Heb. ii. 14. Cf. Rev. vii. 16, 17, R.V. " For the
Lamb shall be their Shepherd and shall guide them unto Fountains
of Water of Life." See p. 180, note 3.
  [1] P. 252, note 3.

Which, when seven days old,
Can young beget,
So, each seventh day, the Saints
Beget disciples,
Who practising the Faith
Obtain Salvation's fruits—
Likeness to God and His Messiah—
    Without a difference.
Thus, practising with all their might,
Trouble is expelled.
Although they have not perfected
The practice of the Six Perfections,[1]
They are naturally ahead
Of all religious pilgrims,
Being the bravest and the strongest.
If one receives the Doctrine of this Scripture,
And reverently believes it,
    As though seeing God,
Then he becomes like God![2]
The weak in faith is transformed
    Into the strong,[3]
Because of this august Scripture's power.
It is as though this body were endowed
With the endurance of the Immortal,[4]

---

[1] The six Cardinal Virtues are—(a) Charity, (b) Morality, (c) Patience, (d) Energy, (e) Contemplation, (f) Wisdom, which is the highest; cf. p. 112.

[2] 2 Cor. iii. 18 ; Matt. v. 48.

[3] Cf. Mark xiv. 66–72 ; Acts ii. 14–38, iv. 13, 29, 33.

[4] Heb. xi. 27.

And had arrived in Port !
All sins and doubts vanish at once ;
He is able all to help [1]
And yet possess abundant grace
To alleviate the great sorrows of his fellow-
    men !
Still more——he can extensively exhort
Both priests and common people
To recite, copy, reverence, explain,
And practise according to this Law,
And, becoming very merciful,
Widely remove the sorrows of mankind.

    Taking deep root in virtue,
    He can cause the common folk
    To produce the holy fruits ;
    Leaving mortality behind,[2]
    Becoming free like gods ;
    Each one enjoys the ecstasy
    Of communing with God.[3]
This so abundant Grace of God
It is impossible to recompense.
It leads each living soul
To obtain a spirit-power.
Thus you, too, may become truly great
In mercy, and in goodness,
Resembling after death the God-like One [4]

---

[1] 2 Cor. xii. 9.
[2] 1 Cor. xv. 54 ; John v. 24 ; Eph. ii. 1, 8.
[3] Ps. xxv. 12–14.   [4] 1 John iii. 2.

Therefore you should extensively
   This Scripture circulate,
And everywhere persuade
All men to learn, recite, copy and perpetuate it.
So doing, you truly are a child of God !

THE ESSENCE OF THE LOTUS SCRIPTURE

[The Text of the Chinese Essence is selected from passages in the Miao Fa Lien Hua King, Nanjio's Catalogue, No. 134, Trans.]

CHAPTER I

Introductory

I have heard
That when all arrangements
For the hearing of the Law [1]
Were ready and complete,
The disciple Adjnata,
The King of Maghadha,

---

[1] It is noteworthy that Augustine on his arrival in Britain, *cir.* 59, wrote to Gregory the Great at Rome about the Royal Island called of old Glascon (*i.e.* Glastonbury), where "the first disciples of the Catholic Law found an ancient Church, prepared by God Himself, . . . to which they adjoined another Oratory, etc. The earlier Church was a wattled cell (by tradition) said to be founded by Joseph of Arimathea, who planted the Faith in Britain in the first century. But the term "Law" is very interesting as indicating a connection between "the Catholic Law" which spread to the Western Ultima Thule in the first ages, and whose traces Augustine found in the sixth century *at the very time* when the Chinese Pilgrim Hiouen Tsang journeyed to India "in search of the Good Guiding Law." See p. 235, note 1.

And an innumerable host
From all the heavens,
And all quarters of the globe,—
God's Angels and the saints of every age
    assembled [1]
To plant the roots of Virtue,
And realise the wish
Of all Illumined ones.

By kindness [2] practising
Divine Wisdom to attain.
God's great Wisdom [3] to comprehend,
And thus in Heaven arrive.

Then kneeling first at Buddha's feet,
Seated in rows, they listened
Whilst He explained to His disciples
    The Mahayana Faith [4]
    The script of boundless, everlasting Right-
        eousness,
And taught the method of discipleship
Which God blesses.

To enjoy the ecstasy
Of " Boundless Righteousness,"
And absolutely
Be at rest,[5]
Thus these assembled received
    Unprecedented joy,

---

[1] Heb. xii. 22, 23, R.V. and mg. ; Rev. v. 8-11-13.
  [2] Acts x. 38.   [3] Rom. ii. 33.
  [4] Heb. i. 1-14.   [5] John xiv. 27.

As with palms folded and
With united heart God they beheld
Down from the lowest hell
Up to the highest heaven
    His Voice they heard.
Sacred memorials of Him
Are raised in the Seven Pagodas.[1]
Sweet incense delights all hearts [2]
As God's Law shines,
Illuminating all living souls.[3]
Though we see ordinary men,
Because of age, decay, and death,
    Surfeited with grief;
We see the Saints encountering
    All kinds of trials

---

[1] Rev. i. 4, ii. 13-20.

[2] Incense was an integral part of worship from the earliest days of man upon earth. It is mentioned both on the Creation and Deluge tablets of Babylonia :

"Daily the God thou shalt worship with offering, prayer and
    incense.
Towards thy God thou shalt have purity of heart,
This is the due of Godhead."

Cf. Matt. ii. 11 ; and in the Liturgy of St. Mark: "The Priest before the Gospel offers incense and saith thus :
"We offer incense before Thy glory, O God, do Thou receive it to Thy holy and supercelestial and intellectual altar. Do Thou *in its stead* pour down the grace of the Holy Spirit." Because this "Incense is offered on account of the grace of the Holy Ghost, which by means of the Gospel was given to the whole world." See Introduction to Neale and Littledale's *Translations of the Primitive Liturgies of the Eastern Church.*

[3] 2 Cor. iv. 3-6.

For preaching Immortality,[1]
Yet hearts and minds
  Are full of joy
Because they seek God's Wisdom.[2]
We also see their knowledge deep,
And spirit strong, able to probe and follow
The Wisdom of all Illumined Ones.
We also see the sons of God
Possessing grace to suffer wrong,
Increasing insults, even to
Buffettings and blows.[3]
Patiently enduring all,
That they may follow in the Way of
  God [4]
Those who " draw near " [5] to Wisdom,
With their might, " put off " [5] distractions,
  Unceasingly rejoice [6]
  Seeking the Highest Way.
Again, we see the sons of God
Have hearts unoccupied.
With this mysterious Wisdom,
They seek the Highest Way.
The limit of their realm

[1] Acts iv. 14–20–29 ; 1 Pet. i. 22–25.
[2] Rom. viii. 35–39.
[3] 1 Cor. iv. 9–12 ; 2 Cor. iv. 7–18, v. 1–4, vi. 4–10, xi. 23–27, xii. 7–9; Phil. i., xii. xiii., R.V.
[4] 1 Pet. ii. 19–23.
[5] Terms adopted from the Ancient Mysteries. See pp. 131, 197, 216, 252 ; Heb. vii. 19, 25, x. 1, 19–21.
[6] 1 Thess. v. 16.

Is the Mystery of Goodness,[1]
  All spiritual forces,
  And rare wisdom.
God seated on His Throne
Presents the Mysterious Law [2]
To such as seek to learn
  And follow It.[3]
Now the World-honoured God
Desires His great Law to make known,
To rain down a great shower of Truth,[4]
To blow a great spiritual Trumpet,
To beat a great spiritual Drum,
To proclaim a great spiritual Righteousness,[5]
To lead all living creatures,
To hear and understand,
And to all the worlds reveal
  This Law
  All human thought surpassing.
Those assembled listeners,
  For thirty hours immovable, together sat
    Listening to God ;
Saying 'twas as the duration of one short meal,
  All this long time
There was not one in mind or body
  Who felt tired.

---

[1] Matt. xiii. 11, 23, 37, 38, R.V. 43, 44; 1 Tim. iii. 16.
[2] Acts ii. 32–36, R.V.   [3] John vii. 17, R.V.
[4] John vii. 37–39 ; Luke xxiv. 47–49 ; Acts i. 8, ii. 4, 17,
21, 33.
[5] Matt. chapters v., vi., vii. See *ante*, p. 131.

In this abnormal state of mind they dwelt ;
It was Divine ; therefore they persevered.[1]

And to-day the Godlike teach
This Mahâyâna Scripture,
Called " the Mysterious Doctrine
Of the Flowering Lotus " ;
Teaching that method of discipling
Which is blessed of God.
Heaven's music is awakened [2]
When man's soul finds rest,[3]
    Seeking the Highest Way.
One must exert all mental effort,
Set free from all attachments,[4]
As 'tis most difficult to attract the Illumined
        Ones.
Only in rare intervals are they met

---

[1] Acts ii. 42, 46, the word here rendered "continued steadfastly"
is translated in Eph. vi. 18, perseverance.

[2] On their arrival at the Interpreter's house John Bunyan makes
his Pilgrim exclaim : " A noise of Music for joy that we are here
. . . . wonderful ! Music in the House, music in the heart, and
music also in Heaven, for joy that we are here ! " It will surely
be noted by the reader that *Joy* and *Music* are the keynotes of
this Lotus Scripture as they are of the Evangelic message of the
New Testament. Most beautifully, also, Dante describes how in
accordance with the " use " or custom of the Holy Hill—"the
religion of the Mountain"—that whenever a disciplined soul
reaches the summit of the Healing Mount of Purgatory and is
received back into the Paradise from whence it came, the whole
mountain vibrates with sympathetic joy, and all the spirits down
to its sea-washed base with one voice cry, " Gloria in Excelsis."

[3] Luke xv. 7, 10, 25.

[4] The grace of " detachment " has always been much insisted on
by all Christian doctors of the Higher Life.

Of clearest Vision,
When the mind grasps all.
I saw the Illuminator
In the midst of the lamps,[1]
Whose Glory thus shone forth.
From Him I learned that He
Desires to make this Living Scripture
    known,[2]
Which is as crystal pure,
The root of all Illumined Ones' good deeds.
Now GOD sheds forth His Light
And manifests true Righteousness.
This all men should know,
Receive with folded palms,
For GOD showers down His Law like
    rain [3]
To satisfy religious seekers—
All seekers—in the three Schools ; [4]
If they have any doubts
GOD will clear them all away.[5]

---

[1] Rev. i. 12–16, ii. 1, iv. 5, "lamps of fire," R.V., v. 6.
[2] Rev. xx. 12, xxii. 19.
[3] Deut. xxxii. 1–3 ; Hos. xiv. 4, 5.
[4] The Hinayana, the Middle, and the Mahâyâna Schools.
[5] "Questionings," Luke xxiv. 15–17, 38–43, R.V. ; John xx.
24–31.

Chapter II

The Art of Saving the World

The Gate of Wisdom, of Good Works,
Is difficult to find and enter.[1]
The knowledge and vision of the Godlike One
Far reaching is and deep,
His tones are gentle,[2]
The heart of all delighting,
What GOD has wrought—
Is most extraordinary,
And difficult to explain;[3]
Only GOD and the Illumined
Can understand It fully.
The true Reality, which we term " Law,"

> Such as form, such as nature,
>
> Such as appearance,
>
> Such as force, such as action,
>
> Such as cause, such as effect,
>
> Such as fruit, such as reward,

[1] Matt. vii. 12–14.

[2] Dante lays much stress on the tones of the voice of the angelic messenger Beatrice, the expression of the eye, the touch of the hand, the smile, etc. etc., and refers to "the healing power the hand of Ananias took" (Acts ix. 12, 17, 18). So, also, it was evidently by the tone of His voice that Mary Magdalene recognised our Lord when He appeared to her as a stranger in another form —that of a gardener, after His rising. Cf. John xx. 15, 16, and x. 3, 5.

[3] 1 Tim. iii. 15, 16 ; Rom. x. 20, R.V.

Such as the history of all things
And of Life's foundations,[1]
One should know this is "Living Seed,"[2]
.The rest is chaff![3]
The language of all the Illumined
Regarding it is one.
When GOD speaks one should repose
Great trust in Him.[4]
The World-honoured Law is ancient,[5]
One must speak of It correctly.
Fold your palms reverently,
To show your wish to hear the Way
More fully.
Pause again, and yet again
Consider, for
My Law is profound, beyond imagining [6]
If one desires to lead all living souls
To understand the Doctrine of the Illumined
And thereby Holiness attain,
And manifest it to the world;[7]
If one desires to instruct all living creatures
In the knowledge of GOD,
And manifest it to the world;

---

[1] To the Hebrews Tôrah, the Law, instruction means "the Foundations of Life."

[2] Matt. xiii. 37, 38, v. 44.

[3] Luke x. 42.   [4] Ps. xxvii., xlvi.

[5] Job xv. 18-22, xx. 4-8 ; 1 John ii. 7 ; Luke xi. 42, R.V.

[6] John i. 1 ; Job ii. 7-9 ; Rom. x. 6-13.

[7] Col. i. 26, 27 ; 1 Tim. iii. 9, 13, 15, 16, R.V. ; 1 John i. 1-3 ; John xvii. 6, 18.

If one desires to lead all creatures
To understand Divine Wisdom
And manifest it to the world;
If one desires to lead all creatures
To enter on the Path of GOD
And make It manifest on earth—
Thou should'st know, Sariputra,
There is but ONE GREAT CAUSE [1]
Enlightening every Sage and Prophet
Manifested in the world!
Oh, Disciples, men and women,
If there be any harbouring contempt,
Troubled with wrongful thoughts,
And unbelievers—therefore—
Cannot make It known
Because they have not grasped the Knowledge—
Now is your opportunity to decide,
And proclaim the Mahâyâna Doctrine.

    In all the universe
    There is but one Doctrine,
    There can be no second nor third,
    Beyond preaching GOD's Goodness; [2]
    The rest are merely symbols—
    Shadows of the True. [3]
    In one word, 'tis not the Lesser Vehicles
    Which can deliver you.

[1] 1 Thess. i. 9, 10 ; Heb. iii. 12 ; 1 Tim. iv. 10.
[2] Ps. xxxiii. 5, cvii.
[3] Heb. viii. 1, 2, 5, ix. 11, 23, 24, x. 1.

I made a vow to save all men,[1]
As each Enlightened One has done
In our Ancient Mahâyâna Vows;[2]
And now, the Way of Deliverance complete,—
All men may find the Path to GOD.[3]
All Law comes from one Source,
Always from the Eternal.[4]
The sons of GOD, practising this Way.
Shall, after Death, become immortal.
Whoever calls upon the Name of GOD,[5]
GOD'S Way has found already.
Of these who hearken and obey,
There is not one who shall not thus
    Become Immortal![6]
There is the Throne of Law Eternal
Which regulates all things in the worlds.
Law-breakers and unbelievers
Fall into all forms of sin.
If one companions with Disciples[7]
In uprightness and goodness,

---

[1] Herein lies the Root-difference between the first Buddhist teachings—those of Shakya and the Hinayana School, B.C. 500, and those of the Mahayana, the New and Greater Way—expressed briefly in two words "Self," "Not-self," being thus in perfect accordance with St. Paul—"No longer I but Christ," Gal. ii. 20, v. 24, the self-negation taught by Christ.   See p. 131.

[2] Rom. ix. 1–4, x. i; Phil. ii. 5–11; 1 John iii. 16.

[3] Heb. ix. 7–15, x. 19–21.

[4] Jas. i. 12, iii. 13–17.

[5] Rom. x. 12, 13, 16; Acts ix. 13, 14—"Saints . . . . all that call upon Thy Name."

[6] John i. 9–18.   [7] Luke xxiv. 13–36.

Discoursing only of the Highest Way,
Learning, rejoicing, and praising GOD,[1]
Their converse is of serving GOD,[2]
And all the Enlightened.[3]
. The generation of the wicked
Hear only the Doctrine of one School.
Being deluded, they disbelieve,
Break the Eternal Law,[4]
Thus falling into hell.

CHAPTER III

Allegories—The World on Fire

Fold the palms of your hands together,[5]
Let body and mind repose,
Then you will quickly attain rest,
And receive a portion of GOD'S Law ;
Your heart will become as peaceful as a lake,
Perfectly straightforward, guileless.[6]
When your mind is made up,
Then in a moment, by repentance
All is done !

[1] Luke ii. 13.

[2] Mal. iii. 16 ; Acts iv. 29–33 ; Heb. xiii. 8.

[3] Heb. xiii. 8 ; Rev. i. 8.

[4] Ps. i. 6 ; Rom. ix. 22 ; Matt. xiii. 13–15 ; Jude 12, 13 ;
1 Tim. iii. 6.

[5] This is one of the Buddhist ways of showing reverence. Cf.
Tit. ii. 2, R.V. "reverent in demeanour."

[6] Isa. lvii. 15 ; Luke xix. 2–10 ; John i. 47–51.

For all one's past and present efforts
And study of God's works
All lead back to God.[1]
This illustrated:
    There is but one Gate,[2]
    There is a great Power
    Working for Peace and Uprightness,
    And for this end there are
    Seven great and precious Chariots,
    Infinite in their dimensions.
One must empty his heart to receive each one.
    The first is: " Great mercy and tenderness;"
    The second: " Untiring perseverance ;"
    The third: " Ever seeking good ; "
    The fourth: " Benefiting others ;"
    The fifth: " Immeasurable gifts ; "
    The sixth: "Rest and joy ;"
    The seventh: " By this Religion one is rid
        Of all sorrow,
    In the three realms."
Yet travelling in these chariots
Throughout the world, in all directions,
Men find no rest.
For this world is like a house on fire,[3]
Full of all kinds of griefs most fearful.
Always there is birth, old age, sickness,

[1] Phil. ii. 13.   [2] 1 Tim. ii. 5.
[3] Cf. 1 Pet. iii. 12. Dean Farrar renders " Make yourselves at home in the conflagrations " ; "think it not strange, etc.," of 2 Pet. iii. 10–12.

Death, and their accompanying sorrows.
Such fires burn unceasingly.
But I have already left the world
With burning habitations,
And dwell in peace and calm,
Resting in shady groves
    In Paradise.[1]
Still in this world I also dwell;[2]
In it all creatures are My children;
Here are countless troubles,
And I alone can save;[3]
Mounting these precious Chariots,
Make straight for the Place
Where true Religion is taught.
For unbelievers in the end
Shall endure hell's anguish;[4]
But those who study Wisdom,
Hear high droctrines.
Ever cultivating a tender heart,
They fear not death nor suffering,
Renouncing all false teaching.
Cultivating the society of good friends—
They are without anger,
Of gentle disposition,

---

[1] John xiv. 1–3. Sukhavati.
[2] Matt. xviii. 20 ; Acts ii. 47.
[3] " And besides Julai (the Model Come) there was found no one who could save," is a phrase occurring in a Sutra translated into Chinese by Ton Hing in A.D. 679.
[4] Mark xvi. 16.

In all things diligent,
Reverencing all the Illumined,
Rejoicing instruction [1] to receive
In the Mahâyâna Scriptures ;
Thus they will not accept
One verse of other Scriptures.[2]

CHAPTER IV

Faith

[Based on Fatherhood]

Greatly congratulate yourself,
You are receiving Treasures inestimable,
Priceless pearls—without the seeking.
Leaving your father's home,
Not knowing where to go,
And adding to poverty—distress.
Your heart repents and thinks of the
Gold, silver, precious stones,
Of which your treasury was full,
You find the Highest Treasure,
Fatherhood,[3] all unsought,[4]

[1] 2 Pet. i. 5–10.
[2] Eph. iv. 11–16 ; 2 Pet. ii. 1 ; 2 John 7–11 ; 1 Tim. vi. 3, R.V.
[3] Luke xv. 11–24 ; John xv. 16.
[4] This expression is very remarkable when compared with St. Paul's words in Rom. x. 20, R.V. : "Isaiah is very bold, and saith, I was found of them that sought Me not ; I *became manifest* unto them that asked not of Me."

Inheritance, and slaves,
And many people—all your own,
In gratitude for GOD's mercy
    Who with kindness
    Won our hearts,[1]
We through long nights
" Lay hold " of God's commands,
And begin to be rewarded, receiving
Great grace from the World-honoured One.[2]
GOD, with rare wonder, pities, instructs
    And blesses us.
Reverently we worship Him who is on high,
Offering Him all things
In the one chariot of Salvation,[3]
Which may be divided into three—
    The elementary (Hinâyana),
    The middle (Madhyimayana),
    And the advanced (Mahâyâna).

CHAPTER V

Medicinal Parables

Since one Earth produces all heroes,
And one rain waters them,
The unsaved may be saved,

[1] 1 John iv. 10, 19 ; Eph. iv. 32 ; Tit. iii. 3, 4.
[2] See p. 99, note 2.
[3] Rom. xii. 1, 2.

The dullard understand,
The weary ones find rest,
The dead may " live,"
And all rejoice—
Quickly are they revived !
Thus, all living souls
May hear this Law,
And peace obtain,
Afterwards becoming powers for Good,
Rejoicing in Religion,
That they may learn the Law of GOD.
Having found the Law,
Of blindness they are cured
In all their ways.[1]
According to their capacity,
Gradually they find the Way of GOD.
The Lord—Breaker of Traditions— [2]
Himself to this world came ; [3]
These important matters studied long
Ere making known His thoughts
To lead all men from bondage,
And rest and joy obtain—
The joy of this world,
And that of Life Eternal [4]

---

[1] *I.e.* they become enlightened or illumined.   Acts xxvi. 16–19 ;
Eph. v. 8 ; Col. i. 12–14.
[2] Mark ii. 23–28, iii. 1–5, vii. 1–13 ; Luke xi. 37, 38 ; Matt.
xv. 2–6–9 ; Luke xiii. 10–17.
[3] John ii. 14 ; Phil. ii. 5–9 ; Heb. ii. 9, 10, 14, 15.
[4] Matt. xix. 29 ; 1 Tim. iii. 8.

The sweet dew of purest Law,[1]
In spirit levelling all castes
To an equality ;
Without a difference of love or hate,
Without covetousness or friction [2]
Again, all the sons of GOD
Stay their whole mind and heart
Upon the Way of GOD,
Ever manifesting kindliness,
Knowing that 'tis Divine ! [3]
The Spirit of the Law is ministered
According to their ability.[4]
What they practise is
   The Way of Saints,[5]
Gradually qualifying
To become themselves divine !

CHAPTER VI

The Record of the Message

I, the Incarnate Light,[6]
Am not Beelzebub's agent,[7]

[1] Hos. vi. 2, 3.

[2] Philem. 16 ; Acts iv. 31, 32 ; Matt. v. 43–45.

[3] Mic. vi. 8, R.V., a mark of the God-Way man.

[4] Eph. iv. 6–16 ; Rom. xii. 5–8.

[5] Acts ii. 2, xix. 23, xxii. 3, 4, xxiv. 14, xviii. 24–27 ; Matt. xxii. 16.

[6] 1 Tim. vi. 14–16.   [7] Matt. xii. 27 ; Mark i. 23–27.

Although demons and demoniac men
Obey My command,[1]
But am the World-honoured HERO,[2]
The Law-giver of the Enlightened,
Who pities men
And gives Glad Tidings,[3]
Falling like sweet dew,[4]
Allaying fever, giving coolness.[5]
As like a weary soldier [6] returning
From hard campaign am at once
Banqueted by the Great King,
And attained Divine Wisdom
And perfect knowledge.
Laying down My life [7]
Ascending to Heaven,[8]
Where I shall ever help men [9]
Through their boundless sorrows
To keep the Law of GOD.
I and you dwell in a Universe
Of Cause and Effect.[10]

[1] Mark i. 23-27, R.V., iii. 11, v. 6, 7, mg. R.V.
[2] Isa. ix. 1, ii. 6.   "Hero-God" (*Expositor's Bible*, G. A. Smith).
[3] Luke ii.
[4] In the frescoes of the Roman Catacombs, Christ, the Angel of the Dew, is depicted as the Fourth with the Children in the Fiery Furnace.
[5] Mark i. 30-34, 39.
[6] Pss. xxiv. 7-10, lxviii. 18 ; Eph. iv. 7, 12.
[7] John v. 26, x. 10-17, 30.
[8] Eph. iii. 8-10 ; Col. ii. 14, 15 ; 1 Pet. i. 10-12.
[9] Mark xvi. 19, 20.   [10] Gal. vi. 7.

It is My duty now to speak,
And yours to hearken!

CHAPTER VII

Parable of the Eternal City

Supreme and Universal is Thy Knowledge
    Oh, GOD-like One.
Thou seest truths ancient and far-distant
Clear as if to-day.[1]
All the mothers weep [2] for the Founder of the
      Law,
    Their holy King;
Passing from grave to grave,
Finding Him nowhere [3]
Then the sixteen Princes (Apostles ?) [4]
In the might of great mercy,
The suffering world to save determined.
    " Holy Lord, the GOD of Heaven,
      From Shakya's grave comes Shakya's voice [5]
    Always entreating,
    Pity all sufferers.[6]

[1] Heb. iv. 12, 13.
[2] Zech. xii. 10; Luke xxiii. 27, 28; John xx. 11–13; Mark
xvi. 9, 10, R.V.
[3] Matt. xxviii. 1–10.
[4] In China the Rakans (Chinese Lohans) or Chief Disciples of
Buddha are 18, in Japan 16.
[5] John i. 32–34.   [6] Mark xvi. 15.

Reverently we worship Thee,
Dwelling in blessedness.
Before Thee we stand,
Desiring that this blessedness
   By all be shared,
So that we, and they with us,[1]
May enter on the Way of GOD."
The Law of Twelve Causes and Effects,
The Wisdom of the GOD-like One,
Is difficult to believe, or comprehend.
O bid all men, " Be fearless," [2] " Fear not." [3]
And " shrink not back." [4]
You may now arrive,
And enter in.
You who are very tired
May be made very glad—
Such gladness as you never had before.
You can now avoid the evils of this life,
And rest obtain,
This is the Eternal City,[5]
GOD's one Chariot of Salvation,
Into three divided.
Balmy breezes waft sweet incense
From the flowers:
And gentle dews fall on the new comers.
Throughout the Heavenly Places

[1] Heb xi. 40.   [2] John xiv. 27.
[3] Matt. x. 28.   [4] Heb. x. 36–39.
[5] Rev. iii. 12, xxi,

They dwell for ever with their teachers.
There, too, is ever a Spiritual Guide
Of most surpassing Knowledge,
Who understands the deep things of the
    heart [1]
And succours all in trouble.[2]
The City has great Gates, high Towers— [3]
Is filled with men and women
Who at the Holy Place [4] arrived
Aided by the merit of all the Illumined.[5]

This City is spoken of as " Three Chariots,"
But, in reality, there is only
One [6] Chariot of Salvation.

CHAPTER VIII

The Five Hundred Disciples [7]

Five hundred disciples—
A great miracle !
The lost body of the Founder
Appeared clearly,
And flies to heaven
    Like a God ! [8]

---

[1] 1 Cor. ii. 10 ; Rom. viii. 27.   [2] Ps. xlvi. 1–3.
[3] Rev. xxi. 10–12 ; Ps. xlviii. 12–14 : "He will be our Guide
even through death."
[4] Rev. vii. 13–17.   [5] Heb. xi., xii. 1, 22–24.
[6] Eph. i. 10 ; Rev. vii. 13–17.   [7] 1 Cor. xv. 6.
[8] Luke xxiv. 50–52 ; Acts i. 6–11.

After this their wills were strengthened,
And in Wisdom they progressed,[3]
Feeding upon the Twofold Feast
With spiritual joy and meditation [1] glad,
For Life is without end ! [2]
And Law is everlasting.
Inwardly and secretly the disciples
Continued in their New Way like Saints,
But outwardly they followed the Old Way,[3]
For few desired to resign life !
But, in reality, they purified Religion.
Marriage they had renounced,
Desiring only to be transformed.
As drunk with wine [4] they slept,
Not knowing they possessed a priceless
     Treasure
In their inmost robes ;
But now they find their sacred Pearl [5]
The poor should also share.
Their heart was greatly gladdened.
The rich, who possessed abundance,
Were unselfish, and shared
All things in common.[6]
Viewing these treasures, the poor were filled
     with joy ;
Bodies and souls with joy o'erflowed.

[1] Acts ii. 41, 42.   [2] John viii. 51.
[3] Acts ii. 46, 47, xxi. 20, 21, 24.
[4] Acts ii. 12, 13, 15.   [5] Matt. xiii. 45.
[6] Acts ii. 42-47 ; " the Fruit of the Light," Eph. v. 9, R.V.

CHAPTER IX

The Simple made Wise

My aim accomplished,
And all human yearnings satisfied,
Learning the fathomless Secret of the Universe,
And of the GOD Supreme,
And Life Immortal—
All men, to save;
The human Way which lengthens life,
The Divine which more secures,—e'en—
    Immortality![1]
My heart's desire is fully realised,
And, filled with joy unspoken,
I dwell in Peace, in God's own Way,
Which is the Highest—[2]
The Good Law of the Sacred Lotus.
Like a lamp GOD's Wisdom shone.
Hearing my Name[3]
Proclaimed "inheritor among the saints,"[4]
My joy was full,
As though refreshed with dew.

---

[1] "There is a law of health for the body and a law of health for the soul; . . . the two together make up the Law of God," says Professor Israel Abrahams of Cambridge, England, in his *Festival Studies.* 1 Tim. iv. 8; cf. vi. 19; Matt. vi. 33.

[2] Luke ii. 14.   [3] Phil. ii. 10, 11.

[4] Col. i. 12.

CHAPTER X

The Spiritual Guide

Amid such things as these
In the Presence of GOD—
I heard the wonderful Living (Lotus) Scripture
　　Sentence by sentence,
And each thought made me glad.
　　I deliver all to you
　　To receive the Highest Wisdom.
God told Me, the Incarnate Great Physician,[1]
After My Death and Deliverance from
　　Death
That "if any hear"[2] a verse, or sentence,
Of this wondrous Living Scripture,
The thought at once shall gladden him,
And I also will "him give a name"
　　Amongst the Enlightened.[3]
　　All these disciples
Revere the millions of Illumined Ones
Who, in all holy places,

[1] Yakushi, the Great and Good Physician, who opens the eyes of the blind, is frequently found among the images in Buddhist temples of the Mahayana or Self-less School. Cf. Luke vii. 18–22, R.V. : "Art Thou He that cometh ?" *i.e.* Messiah.

[2] This Chinese expression is very common and not easily intelligible in any other sense.

[3] A frequent expression used by our Lord in the Fourth Gospel and in the Revelation.

Perform their great vow
Of saving fellow-beings
Who now are dwelling amongst men.
　　These workers—all the worlds
Should reverently esteem,
They should be reverenced
As people reverence Me ! [1]
Because they descended into an evil world
To practise the Doctrines of this Scripture.
If these good men,
And devout women,
After My Death and Deliverance
Shall to only one soul
Preach this Scripture,
If but one line only,
Know that such an one
Is My messenger [2]
And My ambassador
To execute My Will,[3]
How much more so
When he instructs the multitude !
I, the Great Physician, say
If a man in evil mood
Curses GOD,
His sin is light,
But should he use bad language

[1] Luke x. 16.
[2] Job xxxiii. 23, mg. ; Eph. vi. 20, R.V.   Cf. Philem. 1, 12, 13.
[3] Luke xv. 7.

To curse believing souls at home, or in
    communities,
And to abuse the followers of this good Law,
His sin is greater far,[1]
Still, if he suddenly listen to this Scripture
He shall find the highest wisdom.
Know that such a man
Shall mount to the desired Heavenly Abode.[2]
If a man seek the Way of GOD,
And when in trouble
With reverent, folded palm
Turns to Me,
With countless songs of praise to GOD,
He gains incalculable merit.
But he who loves the study of this Word
Has joy surpassing that.[3]
I, Great Physician, now aver that
Of the many writings I inspired,
This Lotus Scripture is the chief of all.
Of this Scripture
I at present
Am almost jealous,
For, after My Death and Deliverance,[4]
Know that I, the Great Physician,
Declare that
He who recalls it
Chants it with reverence,

[1] Matt. xii. 31, 32.   [2] Luke xxiii. 43.
[3] Ps. cxix.   [4] Acts ii. 24.

Proclaims it to others,
I will
Clothe him again [1]
For other regions;
Where all Illumined Ones support him.[2]
This man has strong faith
And high purpose—
The true root of all Goodness.[3]
Know that this man
Dwells with Me,[4]
I having ordained him
And laid Mine own hands on his head.[5]
All the saints of Highest Learning
Follow this Scripture.
It opens the Gate of Goodness
And explains the True Realities.
The Treasury of this Scripture [6]
Is deep, strong, secret, far—
Far beyond the reach of men.
It connects with My Palace,
Is clothed with My Robes,
He is seated on My Throne.[7]
I, the Great Physician, have other lands

---

[1] Rev. iii. 5.   The Primitive Liturgies speak of the "Vestment of Immortality."   Cf. also Rev. xix. 8, R.V., "the fine linen is the righteous acts of the saints."   See p. 249, note 2.

[2] Rev. iv. 4.

[3] Jas. i. 6–8, 21, R.V. ; Phil. iii. 12–14.

[4] Rom. viii. 9 ; John xiv. 23 ; Rev. iii. 20.

[5] John xv. 16 ; Acts viii. 18 ; Rev. i. 17, 19.

[6] Ps. cxix.   [7] Rev. iii. 21.

Which I am sent to save.[1]

Those who meet to seek the Law are many.

To train disciples,

Men and women,

Inquiring men,

Inquiring women,

Who listen to their Preaching of the Law.

Their followers

Listen, and believe,

Obey without resistance.

If the Preachers

Are in quiet places,

I constantly send

Dragons and demons,

The powers of the Air,[2]

Asuras, and such-like,

To listen to their preaching;

Although I dwell in other lands,

I ofttimes give the Preachers

A vision of Myself.[3]

Should any wish to lose their weariness

    To dwell with Me,

---

[1] John x. 16 ; 1 Pet. iii. 18, 19.

[2] Job i. 6–8 ; John xii. 31 ; Eph. ii. 2, iii. 8–10, R.V. : "That now unto the principalities and the powers in the heavenly places might be made known *through the Church* the manifold Wisdom of God." Cf. 1 Cor. iv. 9, R.V., "a spectacle unto the world, both to angels and men." Also Eph. vi. 12, R.V. "the spiritual hosts of wickedness in the heavenly places." Also Judg. v. 20, mg.

[3] Mark xvi. 19, 20 ; Acts vii. 55, xxii. 17–21, xxvii. 23. Cf. also Acts xxiii. 11 with 2 Tim. iv. 16, 17.

Bid them hearken to this Scripture.[1]
Those who have not heard this Word
Are far from Divine Wisdom.
But the House of My messengers, My dwelling-
    place,
  Is filled with mercy;
My Robes are gentleness and long-suffering,
My throne is in the unseen Eternal Land.
They sit on unseen thrones.[2]
If when preaching this Word
There should be men of evil tongue blaspheming,
Bearing swords and spears, or throwing stones,
If, after My death and Deliverance,
There be some able to preach this Scripture,
I will send them forth
To disciple men and women,
And faithful followers win,
To reverence the Holy Spirit,
Who leads all living creatures
And gathers them to hear the Law.
Should any desire to work them ill
By sword, or spear, or stones,
I will send men to tame them,[3]

---

[1] Matt. ii. 28.

[2] Resembling the fire in *Pilgrim's Progress*, which, although deluged with water, burned brightly on owing to the secret supplies of oil continually added by Unseen Hands.

[3] 2 Pet. ii. 12–22, R.V. "Tame," *i.e.* civilised men "born mere animals." The eighth of Buddha's ten titles is Câstâ devâ Manu Shyânâm—"the Tamer of all beings"; and it is interesting to note that the Greek word παλεια translated in our English Bible

And will protect My messengers.
If you " draw nigh " the Holy Spirit,
You will find the Way of Saints ;
When, following the teaching of this Guide,
You will discover innumerable Enlightened
Ones.[1]

CHAPTER XI

God's Dwelling-place (Pagodas) [2]

There are seven Shrines,
Facing the four points of the compass.
From the midst of these
A great voice rises,[3]
Crying, " Holy, holy ! " [4]

"chastened" means originally to bind, then to tame, then to
chastise, and then to instruct. Cf. Ps. xxxii. 8, 9. Thus Pere
Didon says of St. Jerome, "the uncouth Dalmatian, the fiery
youth intoxicated awhile by pagan Rome, became a lion tamed at
the feet of Christ." And, again, Dr. Alex. Whyte has written of
St. Teresa that "all her life through she was as a lioness pallisaded
round by crosses until by means of them she became transformed into a lamb." Cf. Mark v. 3, "tame," A.V., Luke viii.
28, 35.

[1] Heb. xii. 22, mg. 23, R.V.

[2] Pagodas are not merely holy places where relics are enshrined
and the Scriptures are treasured, but seven gates (Churches ?) to
the heavenly city.

[3] Rev. v. 11, "A voice of many Angels," R.V.

[4] Isa. vi. 3 ; Rev. iv. 8. The Trisagion or Tersanctus is found
in every one of the Primitive Liturgies : "the copy of things in
the Heavens." In that of St. Mark it is called "the holy hymn
of the Quickening Trinity."

Sâkyamuni,[1] the world-reverèd One,
At the great Council was enabled
To reveal the Way of Saints,
The GOD-inspired,
The wondrous Lotus-Scripture,
Which He reveals to all
In such wise as this:
" I, the world-honoured One,
Speak words
All which are true,
These great Shrines
Are spiritual *ferry-boats*[2] to the Promised Land;
People call them precious Arks.[3]
In them GOD is revealed,
Hence they are, also, called
      His precious jewels.[4]
Throughout all worlds,
Where'er the Living Word is preached,
It is My Shrine.[5]
This Scripture being therein heard
Reveals to those thus gathered

[1] Kern says he had not the slightest doubt that by "Sâkyamuni" here is meant the Supreme Being, God of gods, Almighty and All-wise (*Sacred Books of the East*, vol. xxi. Introduction, p. 28). See p. 226, note 6 ; p. 248, note 3.

[2] A term descended from the Pyramid-age. Max Müller says that the Mahayana means "the School of the Great Boat."

[3] Or "the Lotus of the Pyramids." In Japan the Mikoshi in Shinto temples is the equivalent, *i.e.* the God-carriage in which the Shintai or token of the God's presence rests.

[4] Mal. iii. 17.

[5] Rev. v. 8–14, or Sanctuary ; cf. 2 Cor. vi. 16, R.V. mg.

Its testimony, therefore they praise,
And Holy, Holy chant.
From all points of the compass—
Above, below—
All regions are transformèd—
Countless millions of distant worlds." [1]
A hush fell upon them all. [2]
They offered gifts of sweetest flowers.
Then Sâkyamuni, with His right-hand Finger, [3]
Opened the seven seals,
And there came forth a great sound
Like the turning of a Key [4]
Opening a great City-gate.
Then all beheld
Two GOD-like ones
Receiving a great assembly
In the open sky. [5]
The Vision seemed as though upon a cool
        Lake-shore
Beside the glorious Lotus.
And a mighty wind rushed [6]
Through the branches of the trees.
From the beginning until now,

---

[1] John xiv. 2.
[2] Rev. viii. 1.
[3] Cf. Ezek. viii. 19, xxxi. 18 ; Dan. v. 5 ; Luke xi. 20 ; John viii.
[4] Like the opening of the seven seals, Rev. iv. 1–5, v. 1–10,
xv, 5–6, xx. 11–15 ; also " the Amen with the Keys " of Life and
Death and " of the Kingdom of Heaven "—Matt. xvi. 19 ; Rev. i.
18.
[5] 1 Thess. iv. 16.   [6] Acts ii. 2, iv. 31.

"Among the many Scriptures circulated,—
This Scripture is the chief.
This Scripture is difficult to follow.
If followed, even temporarily, I rejoice,—
All the Illumined Ones rejoice.[1]
For such men pleased the Illumined,
They are brave, progressive,
Well disciplined.
Those who quickly gain
The Way of GOD supreme,
Can after death this Scripture study,
More and more.
They truly are the sons of GOD,
In perfect goodness dwelling.
After My Death and Deliverance
They can better understand its meaning.[2]
The Messengers of Heaven are as eyes
To this awe-full world,
And can make it plain.
These Messengers of Heaven
Should be revered
Because they teach those who suddenly
Attain the highest Way of GOD."

[1] In the Primitive Liturgy of St. Clement these words occur:
"Pray ye that are Illuminated! For our newly illuminated
brethren, let us make our supplication that the Lord may confirm
and strengthen them. Let us, the faithful, all pray earnestly for
them, that the Lord may count them worthy, having been initiated
into the death of Christ . . . . and sharers of His Mysteries,"
etc. See *ante*, p. 175, note 1.

[2] Cf. Luke xxiv. 5, 6 ; John ii. 19–22.

Chapter XII

The Converted Persecutor [1]

Diligently practice philanthropy;
Be not stingy:
Spare not thy body nor thy life,
The people of this world
May attain Eternal Life!
I have the Mahâyâna Doctrine
Called "The Lotus Scripture."
If in obedience.[2]
You constantly proclaim it—
Whether gathering fruit,
Or drawing water,
Collecting wood to cook a meal,
Or lying down, or sitting up,
Unwearied you will be
In mind and body.
Although the world is mine
I covet not its pleasures,
For I possess a wondrous Secret,[3]

[1] Deva was a disciple of Nagarguna (Nanjio). Like Saul becoming Paul, Acts xxii. 13, 25.

[2] St. Paul "not disobedient to the Heavenly Vision," Acts xxvi. 19.

[3] It is said that Keikwa, a famous Chinese sage, communicated to Kōbō Daishi, the young Japanese priest who was sent over to Singanfu in A.D. 804, "a wonderful Secret." It was the doctrine of Dainichi, the Great-Everywhere-Present-Sun (see p. 256, note 4). On his return to Japan, Kōbō Daishi founded the Shingon sect, and Dengyc Daishi, his colleague, founded the Tendai sect of Mahâyâna

Known only to the few.

Possessing It,

My mind and body are unwearied.

Golden, purple-coloured.

All-powerful, fearless,

Having a binding power

To persecute the Saints—

Lo! by miracle

I was converted to the True Way.[1]

Buddhism, which regard the Lotus Scripture as the basis of his faith. Kōbō Daishi united Buddhism and Shintoism in the system called "Ryobu Shinto" (which lasted until forty years ago, 1868, the Meiji era); transformed the rude Shinto Bird-perch into the beautiful Portal called Torii, doubtless in allusion to "the Gateway of Light" and the "Luminous Temples" which he had seen in Singanfu, while the Chinese Emperor gave him a box of which the central ornament was the Maltese cross which is on the Nestorian inscribed stele at Singanfu. Kōbō Daishi also baptized the Japanese Emperor Saga into Dainichi and wrote for him a "Key to the Secret Treasure House." It is surely extremely significant that the mitre worn by the priests of the Shingon sect when receiving baptism is adorned in front with five figures arranged in the form of the same Maltese cross. The central figure being that of Dainichi, the "Jesus our Immanuel" of Christians supported by Shakya and Amida, above and below being figures symbolising Wisdom and "the Precious Birth," clearly the New Birth of St. John's Gospel iii. 3, 5; by which the early believers receiving baptism became φοτισμος, "Enlightened Ones." The baptismal robes are most glorious crimson brocade, interwoven with shining gold. The curious designs thereon having been handed down from Keikwa (or Huikō) and Kōbō Daishi 1100 years ago. See p. 227, note 3.

[1] Acts ix. 1–19. A frequent expression in the Acts of the Apostles. See Revised Version, where it is accentuated by a capital W "Way." Acts ix. 2, xix. 9, xxii. 4, xxiv. 14, 22, xviii. 25–28. Shinto or Kami no michi, the Way of the gods. "I am the Way," John xiv. 6.

GOD says to all His followers,
And to those as yet unborn,—
If good men
And devout women,
Hear this Living Scripture
Of the Persecutor,
With clean heart and reverent faith,
Free from doubts
They will not descend to Hades.
E'en hungry ghosts and animals [1]
May attain to the Court of Heaven,
Dwell with the Illuminate
And always hear this Scripture.
Whether dwelling among men, or with the
      Angels,
They will alike enjoy abundant bliss,
If in GOD'S Presence
They remain and grow.
And in a little while,
E'en in the islands of the sea—
I will reveal to them
This marvellous Scripture.
   " When only eight years old
   I pitied all the creatures
   As though new-born babes—
   Treating them with kindness
   Bent on peace and gentleness.

---

[1] 2 Pet. ii. 12, R.V. "born mere animals"; cf. Ps. xxxii. 8, 9;
1 Cor. xv. 44, 45.

In all kinds of suffering
I cultivated virtue."
Before finishing this speech,
An Angel [1] then appeared
Saying he had heard
I had attained Divine Wisdom,
It needed only that GOD Himself confirm it.
I continued studying the Mahâyâna Law [2]
Which saves all men from suffering.
I heard that
The form of woman is unclean,
Is not a spiritual vessel,
And that she has
Five disqualifying drawbacks :—
The first, she could not attain to heavenly
 royalty :
(Second) could not become GOD'S Prophet ;
(Third) could not control the evil spirits ;
(Fourth) neither become Director of trans-
 migration ;
(Fifth) nor attain unto the form of God.
 But there is a precious Pearl—
 Worth a million worlds—
 Which suddenly can
 Change her into a child of GOD,
 Reigning for ever on the Precious Lotus-
 Throne,

[1] Cf. Rev. i. 20, ii. 1 with Acts vii. 38, ix. 10–17, 26, 27.
[2] *I.e.* the Inner Doctrine of the Greater Way.

Perfect in knowledge.
The whole assembly pondered thoughtfully
And believed this Message.

CHAPTER XIII

" Hold Fast ! " [1]

Afterwards, the evil world multiplied.
Goodness diminished,
Conceit abounded,
Love of money was supreme,[2]
Evil increased,
And men drifted [3] far from GOD.
Though difficult, yet still they may be taught.
We should brace our minds to great En-
     durance—
Determine to study and recite this Scripture,
To preach and copy it—
In every way to reverence it—
Sparing no pains, nor even life itself.
In this bad world
Most men are evil,
Cherishing conceit.[4]

[1] "Hold Fast," a term from the Mysteries, Rev. ii. 13, 25, iii. 11.   See pp. 151, 161, 251.
[2] Cf. 2 Tim. iii. 1-5 ; 1 Tim. vi. 10, R.V.
[3] Heb. ii. 1, R.V., " drift away " ; 2 Pet. ii. 17, R.V.
[4] 1 Tim. iii. 6, vi. 4 ; 2 Tim. iii. 3, vi. 10, R.V.

Their goodness is a sham.[1]
Angry, coarse, slippery, and crooked,
Because untrue in heart.
Still—thanks to the great Holy Spirit,[2]
Who gradually prepares to tread the Way of
    GOD—
Some reverently obey His Mind,
Are brave as lions,
Travel anywhere,
To any quarter of the earth[3]
The Doctrine to explain;
Practising it in their lives,
And pondering over its true meaning—
All through the wondrous power of GOD![4]
There are many ignorant men
Cursing, blaspheming,
Carrying swords and spears—
But all these things must be endured,
For the followers of an evil world
Are ignorant.[5]
Their hearts are slippery and crooked,
Not having got what is to be obtained
Their heart is filled with pride.
Some ascetics

[1] Matt. xiii. 20, 21 ; Hos. vi. 4.
[2] Neh. ix. 20, "Thou gavest Thy Good Spirit to instruct them"; Rev. iii. 6.
[3] Matt. xxiv. 14 ; Acts i. 8.
[4] Heb. ii.
[5] 1 Cor. xv. 9 ; 2 Cor. ii. 7–12, iv. 9–14.

Retire with monkish garb [1]
Dreaming that thus they follow the true
    Way.
Despising others,
These cherish ill,
Ever following the customs of the world,
Falsely they call themselves " disciples."
To rid them of their sin,
Making a doctrine of their own,[2]
Madly deceiving people,
Ministers of State,
Brahmins, students,
And all disciples,
Us they calumniate with evil speech.
We therefore worship GOD,
Enduring all this wrong,
Regarding them as froth—
For all we are gods ! [3]
So with highest words
We should endure.[4]

    Amidst an evil world
    There are many fears
    Lest evil spirits should possess us,
    Curse us, and disgrace us,
    Hence should we reverently believe in GOD
    And don the breastplate of Endurance,

---

[1] " Wolves—in sheep's clothing," Matt. vii. 15.
[2] 1 Tim. iv. 1–3 ; Rom. xvi. 17, 18.
[3] Cf. John x. 34, 35.   [4] Acts iv. 19, 20.

That we may make this Scripture known,
And suffer all afflictions.

CHAPTER XIV

Peace and Joy

Those who endure insults,
Are gentle and obedient,
Not proud nor fearful,
Meditating solely upon GOD
And this world's vanity,
Speaking but little,
Wishful to know first the elements of Truth,
Then all the Buddhists,
Without distinction,
These men and these women,
Possessing all truths
Still have none !
Have no abiding
And are eternally so,
Yet dwell in perfect rest,
Like the Himalaya peaks,
Meditating upon right learning.
In order to direct their thoughts
To follow Righteousness — and see Unseen
        Things— [1]

[1] 2 Cor. iv. 16–18.

Then the heart would be at rest
Without any weakness,
Not discussing others, or their faults.
There are problems
Which the elementary Hina school cannot
    solve.
Only the advanced Maha can explain
Or comprehend deep wisdom.
Having washed away uncleanness,[1]
Put on clean garments,
Becoming pure within, without—
Are quietly seated on unseen thrones [2]
From all trouble freed.
Then, with kind heart thus making known
    the Law,
By night and day proclaim
Religion's highest Way.

[1] Both Buddhists and Shintoists rinse their mouths and wash their hands before offering prayer; and pilgrims change their clothes and sandals before approaching the Shrine; see Gen. xxxv. 2, 3 ; Ex. xix. 10, 11. So, also *cir.* A.D. 347, St. Cyril of Jerusalem in his mystical Catechism says: "Ye have seen the Deacon giving water to the Priest to wash his hands, and to the Presbyters who surround the Altar of God. . . . That cleansing of the hands is a symbol that we must be made clean from all our sins and iniquities." (See Ps. xxvi. 6.) And of old the custom was that all who intended to be Communicants should wash their hands. (See Neale and Littledale, *Primitive Liturgies of the Eastern Church*, p. 179, "Office of the Prothesis as performed in the Great Church and the Holy Mountain," and note that all Buddhist temples in Japan are also called "Mountain"—as was this Christian Church as well as the Jewish Temple at Jerusalem. Cf. Isa. ii. 2, 3 ; Ezek. xliv. 10–12 ; Rev. vii. 14.

[2] Rutherford says, "I reign as King over my crosses."

If disciples can proclaim [1]
My wondrous Gospel
Without anger in their heart,[2]
Freed from hindrances and trouble,
Are not fretful: [3]
Indifferent e'en to curses,
Also without fear
Of swords, spears, or stones,
And towards all creatures
Feel a great pity,—
A Father's pity,—
Like the GOD-like Ones—
A teacher's pity,
Like the Saints—
These messengers of GOD
Ever with gentleness preach the Law,
Are rich in mercy
And, in all things,
Ne'er grow heart weary.[4]

Some come to put hard questions,[5]
But all the Angels, night and day,
Because of this Law
Defend them.[6]

If a powerful prince were to arise,

[1] Cf. Acts ix. 20–22, R.V. See p. 141.
[2] Matt. v. 9, 22–24, 43–48 ; 1 Pet. ii. 1–3.
[3] Ps. xxxvii. 1, 7, 8, 34–40 ; Heb. xii. 1.
[4] Rev. ii. 3, R.V.
[5] Luke xii. 11, 12 ; Matt. xxii. 15 ; John iii. 2–4, vi. 30, 42, 52.
[6] Dan. vi. 22 ; Ps. xci. 11 ; Acts xii. 6–11.

Desiring, with all-conquering force,
All Kingdoms to subdue,
And win them to one spiritual Realm,
Under the Chief of the three Realms,
Under the great Eternal King,
Who evermore endureth insult,
All creatures pitying,
Like a royal prince,
Distributes precious gifts.
Most precious of all this Scripture is
Above all Scriptures.
Ever treasure it;
Never forget to publish it—
This is the very time to do so.
He who reads this Scripture
Shall be from sorrow free,
Free from pain or sickness.
His skin shall be fresh and white,[1]
Without disease,
Not mean nor ugly,
But noble-looking, like a saint.
All angels in the heavens
Rejoice to wait on him.[2]
Weapons cannot injure,
Nor poison hurt.[3]
If men curse, their mouths are dumb.
Fearlessly they travel like prophet-princes,

[1] Job xxxiii. 23-25-27.   [2] Mark xvi. 17, 18.
[3] Rom. viii. 31-39.

Their wisdom shineth like the sun.
In dreams they see such wondrous things—
A hundred glorious visions,[1]
Such are their constant dreams,
So that at last e'en ill men say,
" This is the best Religion ! "
Conferring great benefits,
E'en all these fore-named gifts.

CHAPTER XV

Resurrection [2]

There is a great multitude—
Chief singers, leaders, who are called by many
    names—
One is " Upward-movers," [3]
Another, " Travellers-everywhere," [4]
Another, " Pure travellers,"
Another, " Travellers who rest in Peace."
These are Chiefs of multitudes.
The leading Prophets,
The honourable of earth who dwell in peace
    and joy,

---

[1] 1 Kings xix. 4–8 ; Heb. i. 14 ; 2 Kings vi. 17 ; Rev. v. 11.   Cf.
Job xxxiii. 15–17 ; Ezek. i. 1 ; 2 Cor. xii. 2–4 ; Rev. i. 10.
[2] Like the Resurrection, 1 Cor. xv. 12–58.
[3] Cf. Phil. iii. 13, 14, mg. R.V., "the Prize of the Upward
calling."
[4] Acts viii. 4.

With few cares, and fewer ills,
Teaching all unweariedly.
Their arm is strong,
Having great power to endure wrong,[1]
Only seeking the Way of GOD.
Amongst this multitude
I know not one,—
They were a multitude—all saints— [2]
Each with a great history.
You should therefore all put on
Their panoply of progress [3]
And be firm in your resolve.
By the wisdom of all the Illumined,
By the miraculous power of all the Illumined,
By the zealous power of all the fiery prophets,
By the daring power and awful majesty of all
    the Illumined,
You now pass beyond the power of simple faith;[4]
And are prepared to suffer wrong for doing
    good [5]

---

[1] Eph. vi. 10, mg. R.V.   [2] Col. i. 12 ; Acts ix. 13, 14.

[3] Matt. x. 16–20. This idea is one of the most ancient in the world, between 3000 and 4000 B.C. According to Maspero and Budge, the stele [of Pepi of the 5th dynasty of Egypt and the Pyramid of Teta, 6th dynasty, they speak of Khu as the "Shining One" or "Glory" represented by a "Flame of Fire." Cf. Heb. i. 7, 14. Dante had much to tell of these Illumined Ones who appeared as "Flames Incoronate" in Inferno and Purgatorio. Cf. Heb. xi., xii. 1.

[4] Cf. Heb. v. 12–14, vi. 1, 2 ; Eph. iv. 12–14–16, R.V. ; Jas. iii. 13, 14, 18.

[5] 1 Pet. ii. 19, 20, iii. 13–16, iv. 3, 4, 14–16–19.

I, Myself, now comfort all,
Cease, then, from doubts and fears.
All GOD'S words are true,
His Wisdom is Immeasurable,
Subdues the heart of men,
Causing them to desire the Way.
Thus progressing, with all their soul
Desiring Highest Wisdom,
My sons thus
Learn My Way.
Night and day progressing,[1]
Seeking the Way of GOD,
Your mind set on strong faith,
Wisdom ever diligently seeking,
Preaching all kinds of spiritual truth
With fearless mind.
I now tell you this true saying,
With your whole heart [2] you must believe it.
I am come from far
To teach and elevate.[3]
This teaching is the greatest earthly Treasure,[4]
There cannot be a doubt.
By worldly ways it is unstained,
And pure as Lotus on the Lake.[5]
Those skilled in answering objections
Need have no fear.[6]

---

[1] 2 Pet. iii. 18.   [2] Heb. xi. 6.
[3] John i. 18 ; Heb. i. 1-4.   [4] Mark viii. 36.
[5] Matt. v. 8.   [6] Luke xii. 11, 12.

Bent on enduring wrong,
Upright with wondrous goodness,
Should any in regard to this Gospel
Doubt and disbelieve,
They shall be sent the way of evil men.[1]

CHAPTER XVI

Jülai is Alpha and Omega

I am a Secret,
Possess miraculous power.
As I was truly born of GOD,
Like Him My age is Infinite— [2]
Millions upon millions of years.[3]
Even in ordinary affairs
I do the Incomprehensible,
According to necessity
In all places, saying,
My name is various,[4]
My age is various.[5]
Rejoicing in the elements of Faith,

---

[1] John iii. 15, 18, 36.   [2] Rev. i. 8, 14.
[3] Na yen to.   A numeral equal to a thousand million.
[4] Isa. ix. 6, "My Name is Secret—Wonderful."   Cf. Judg. xiii.
18.
[5] "Ancient of Days," Dan. vii. 13. "Babe," "Child," "Boy,"
"Youth," Luke ii. 12, 27, 43, R.V.

Where good deeds are but few
And misdeeds many—
Whether speaking of Myself
Or of others,
Whether directing Myself
Or others,
Whether My own affairs
Or those of others—
Whate'er I say
It all is true.
Wherefore ?
Because I truly see
The spiritual forms of the three Realms
Without birth or death ;
Whether retiring, or coming forth,
I am not of these worlds.[1]
And as to My death and translation,
'Tis neither real, nor unreal,
Not like, yet not diverse,
Unlike the three Realms
But visible in all three Realms.
With these Signs [2]
You see clearly Who I am,
Without mistake !
The Divine works I do
Are not passing illusions.
I am the Truth,[3]

[1] Heb. vii. 15–17.　　　[2] Matt. xi. 3–6.
[3] John xiv. 6.

Who am the Same,[1]
("Yesterday, To-day—For ever,")
Without birth, or death.[2]
The Illumined appear on earth,
But are not quickly recognised.
Since the Beginning when I dwelt with GOD,[3]
Long ages past,
My life unmeasured is—
Through all Kalpas of Time.
I never perish,
The Way of Saints [4] I follow,
Which Life secures for evermore.
My Life is not ended
But multiplied.[5]
I have Medicine
To cure all sicknesses
As GOD, dwelling upon earth.[6]

[1] "The Same"—not only in the Old and New Testaments and Prayer-book, but also in the Egyptian Teaching. The "True Same" of Buddhists, the "Very Same" of Christians. "Yesterday, To-day, For ever" is in the "Book of the Dead" as moderns call the "Book of the Master of the Hidden Place."

[2] Heb. vii. 3 ; Rev. xxi. 6.   [3] John i. 1 ; Prov. viii. 22.

[4] Prov. viii. 20, 21 ; 1 Tim. vi. 12, 19, "Lay hold on the Life which is life indeed," R.V.

[5] Not long ago, a devout orthodox Jew was calling upon a friend of mine on Easter Day. In the course of conversation he remarked, "Do you know I always think that the physical resurrection of Jesus is not so miraculous as His spiritual resurrection, I mean the way in which for 1900 years He has lived in the hearts and lives of countless millions of His followers, in all ages, and in all lands. That to my mind is by far the greatest miracle !"

[6] Isa. liii. 4 mg. R.V. ; Matt. viii. 17 ; Luke vi. 19, ix. 42, R.V., etc.

14

The man of scanty virtue
Not being well rooted in good works [1]
Is poor and mean,
Lusting after all pleasures
Which entice his heart,
Ignoring the net in which he once was
       caught,[2]
Taking poisoned drugs
Which madden him,
He falls upon the ground.
Whether out of his senses,
Or in his right mind,
Trying all kinds of remedies
But deems the best ones bad,
And bad ones " fine, fragrant, tasteful,"
Procures all kinds abundantly
Then, mixing well, he swallows them.
Hence, the Illumined Saints
Send Medicine to their patients,
Seeking all to save.
   True and not false,
   This message send,
And speak these words :
" This Medicine is most excellent,
In colour, taste, and fragrance—
Each and all abundantly—
If you partake
Your troubles soon will flee."

[1] Matt. xiii. 21, 22.   [2] 2 Pet. ii. 9.

No longer will you suffer from your many
     ills.

Seeing this good Medicine,

In colour, fragrance—all so choice,

Partake of it.

Of all disease you will then be cured,

Although the poison may have deeply entered

And destroyed the natural health.

But these beauteous-looking,

Fragrant medicines, though fragrant and sweet-
     tasting,

Are really bad ;

Let Fathers ponder this.

I now found a Society

For doing good,

To make men take True Medicine.[1]

So write I now these words,—

" These are good remedies

Which I now bequeath

For you to take.

Do not vex yourself about their worth,

But cherish constantly a grateful heart.

Then your awakening mind

[1] The Chinese call this the " Pill of Immortality." Cf. John vi.
27, 35.   In A.D. 107 the martyr St. Ignatius of Antioch spoke of
" the medicine of Immortality," alluding to the Holy Eucharist.
St. Thomas Aquinas attributes four effects to Its reception—
" Nourishment or sustentation, growth, repair, delight." Cf. p.
92, note 4.   The Council of Trent declared It to be " the Antidote
by which we are healed of our daily faults and are preserved from
mortal sin."

Will know that this Medicine
Is truly good, beautiful, fragrant, and pleasant-
      tasting;
When you take it
All poisonous sickness will be cured."
Some will ask, " What is
This so-called good remedy,[1]
Is it not trash ? "
I say, " No!
Since I possessed the wish Divine
All men to save,
Good works reveal Eternal Source ; [2]
And truly do I neither die, nor rise again,
But unchangeably remain, preaching Salvation.
Perpetually I exist for this,
With nature straight, and purpose gentle,
I live for ever—and I never die.
Here there is death which is no death,[3]
Drowned in a sea of trouble,[4]
But one desirous GOD to see
Fears neither death nor trouble,
Then I with all the Teachers

[1] Cf. with this the Jews' questionings recorded by St. John
(vi. 52, 60, 66, p. 103, note 1).

[2] "The Same."   John i. 2.   See p. 70, note 2.

[3] "Dying, and behold we live."   2 Cor. vi. 8 ; cf. iv. 8–11, 16 ;
Rev. xiv. 13 ; 2 Tim. i. 10.

[4] "I am not exhausted, I shall not drown. The palm flowers of
Shii—the Light—are over me. Blessed are those that see the
bourne!"   Such are the exclamations of the Pilgrim-soul in the
'Book of the Dead."

Became manifest upon a spiritual mountain,[1]
Being continually there
Besides in other places."
When the end of all things comes
And the last great fire is burning,[2]
I remain in peace in this sphere,
By Angels surrounded,
'Mid gardens, forests, palaces,
And all kinds of glorious things—
Splendid trees,[3] sweet flowers and fruits
Where all creatures wander joyously—
'Mid heavenly choirs resounding—
Constantly making melody.

Dewy wreaths of flowers
Are offered before GOD and the Illumined.
This Pure Land never fades,
And all behold the burning up of trouble,
Fears, and every sorrow.[3]
This Paradise is full of saved ones.
There the Name of the Three Precious Ones [4]
    is not heard,
For there the Light of Wisdom shineth to
    infinitude.[5]
For immeasurable ages [6]
Rejoicing in their heritage.
You who are wise

---

[1] Matt. v., vi., viii.   [2] 2 Pet. iii. 7–13.
[3] Rev. xxii. 1–5.   [4] Rev. vii. 14–17.   See p. 217, note 1.
[5] Note the great similarity between this and Rev. xxi. 22, 23.
[6] Rev. iv. 9.

Doubt not
But decide all to receive for evermore.
Mine are not empty words,
The meek I regard as My deliverers
To save men from all trouble.
Whenever one has this desire
To save and lead all
To reach the Highest Way—
He soon becomes Divine.
But they who constantly behold Me
And yet are proud in heart,[1]
Following their own desires,
Will fall into the way of evil men.
You should try men [2]
Whether they follow " the Way " or not ?
And, as occasion offers, save them
By unveiling to them the deep truths of the
     Spirit.[3]

CHAPTER XVII

Various Blessings

Heaven thunders Its speech,
Far doth the sacred sound resound.
The world-honoured One has power omni-
     potent [4]

---

[1] 1 Tim. iii. 6, R.V.   [2] 1 John iv. 1.
[3] 1 Cor. ii. 3–10, R.V.   [4] Matt. xxviii. 18 ; Rev. xix. 6.

And age immeasurable.

All rejoice,

GOD's Name in every realm is heard.

Forgiving, show'ring blessing on all beings.

Rooting them in good,

Aiding them reach the highest goal.

When all living beings

Heard of GOD's age—

Boundless like this—[1]

They were able to receive Faith [2]

From this one thought, " Clearly

This power of Faith

Immeasurable is."

If, in addition, wrong they could endure,

And in meekness dwell,

E'en were all kinds of insults added,

Their hearts unmoved would be,

Their minds be firmly set

To grow not weary

Nor sleepy, but ever be alert.

For eighty million years

They live on undisturbed,

Treasuring up this bliss within their heart—

They seek the Highest Way,

Obtain all knowledge,[3]

Amid all forms of study.

Still one glimpse of Faith [4]

[1] Rev. xv. 3, R.V., " King of the Ages."
[2] Matt. xvii. 20.   [3] John xvi. 13.   [4] Mark ix. 23.

Surpasses all in happiness.

Holding fast this joy of the heart,[1]

Seeking the Highest Way.

Deeply believe this sudden faith

And its results

That by faith you can obtain them,[2]

So you may all

This Scripture of Immoral Life with reverence accept;

If one truly be sincere,

Holy, straightforward, and reasonable,

He may suddenly grasp it,

Explain the word of GOD,

And, with deep faith, explain the Spiritual

In My presence.

My service is fruitful,[3]

Immeasurable, infinite.

North, South, East, West,

Above, below,

Courageously advancing,

All good possessing,

Rooted [4] in wisdom

And able to answer all questions.

---

[1] A term derived from the Mysteries. See p. 251, note 1 ; also
1 Tim. vi. 12, " Lay hold on the Life eternal " ; also v. 19, " that
Life which is life indeed," R.V.

[2] See Heb. x. 39, mg. ; xi. 1 mg., R.V., " Faith to the gaining
of the soul . . . is the giving substance to—or, substantiates the
things hoped for, the test of things unseen."

[3] John xv. 4, 5, 7, 8.   [4] Cf. Col. ii. 6.

If you "lay hold"[1] of this Immortal Scripture,

It will be as though GOD were present with you;

If free from anger, or evil speech,

And reverent in all places where God meets human souls,[2]

Humble, below all the disciples;[3]

Far from pride,

Reverent in mien and attitude,

Your heart resembling God's own,

Then you will say—

"Let us build temples here[4]

For the sons of GOD to dwell in, in this spiritual state

Let us be used by GOD,

Dwell ever with His children,

And act as though one family."[5]

CHAPTER XVIII

The Blessing of Glad Tidings

[Conversion?]

After My Death and Passing-over,

Those who hear the Doctrine of this Scripture

---

[1] See p. 251, note 1.

[2] Heb. xii. 28, R.V., "Reverence and awe." Cf. 1 Tim. iii. 16, lit. "Great is the Mystery of Reverence."

[3] Mark ix. 34, 35; John xiii. 14, 15.

[4] Matt. xvii. 4.   [5] Eph. iii. 14, 15.

Immediate joy can win ! [1]
And find a spring perennial of bliss
For parents, ancestors and kin—
Glad Tidings for their friends
Seizing occasions to make this Wisdom known
Among all creatures. [2]
Pleasures I grant
According to their wishes
To enjoy abundantly. [3]
The fiftieth man
To whom this Scripture is transmitted—
This hearer receives immediate joy,
Infinite, immeasurable,
And incalculable.
How much greater is the joy
When first heard in the assembly,
Where many are made glad.
Their happiness is greater far—
Immeasurable, infinite,
Incalculable, incomparable ! [4]

---

[1] In A.D. 552, when the King of Korea sent "The Image of the Three Precious Ones" and the Hoke-Kyo or Lotus Sutra to the Emperor of Japan, he wrote a letter commending the most excellent doctrine with Treasure so wonderful—that every prayer is fulfilled to the heart's content. And the chronicle of the Nihongi records that "the Emperor" leaped for joy, saying: "Never until now had we the opportunity of listening to so wonderful a Doctrine ! " Cf. Acts viii. 4–8, 39, xvi. 34, etc.

[2] Mark xvi. 15, R.V., "Preach the Gospel to the whole creation." Cf. Rom. viii. 22, 23.

[3] Cf. Prov. viii. 14–21, 35 ; Acts iii. 6–8.

[4] Luke xxiv. 53.

The joys of this world are unstable,
They are like froth, bubbles, *sparks*.
We speak of the Doctrine of this Scripture
As " deep, mysterious,[1]
Able to save from millions of calamities."
Let the spirit be pure.
Let the robes be fragrant
And speech be always radiating.[2]
How much more must the heart be pure,
The choicest Teachings of this Scripture
    making clear
By speaking and behaving them ![3]
One's blessedness then is infinite.[4]

Chapter XIX

The Blessing of a Spiritual Herald [5]

If good men
And good women
This living Scripture follow, whether
Reading or reciting it,

---

[1] Cf. 1 Cor. ii. 6–8.   [2] Jas. i. 9–18 ; Heb. xiii. 15, 16.

[3] 2 Tim. ii. 21, 22, 24. A Chinese student who was converted when in Japan sent this message to his missionary friend : "Tell Mr. X. I am studying the Bible every day, and *behaving* it."

[4] 2 Pet. ii. 5, mg. R.V. (cf. Heb. xi. 7 ; 1 Pet. iii. 20).

[5] Lit. a public crier ; cf. Jonah iii. 1–5 ; Mark i. 3–5 ; cf. p. 151, note 4.

Explaining or transcribing it,
These men shall receive—
Eight hundred marks for the eye,
Twelve hundred for the ear,
Eight hundred for the nose,
Twelve hundred for the tongue,
Eight hundred for the body,
Twelve hundred for the mind.
For all these good marks,[1]
All faculties most precious,
In all eight hundred eye-marks,
The sight is glorious!
On account of this glory
The eyes are most clear-sighted.[2]
The ears given them by their parents
Are clean without impurity.
Ever with this ear hearkening to
The cries of all the world,
Whether reading or reciting Sacred Books,
Or telling others of them.
The True Preacher dwells there,
And everything can hear,[3]
Down to the depth of hell,
Up to the vault of heaven.

[1] Cf. Gal. vi. 17, R.V.   Dante mentions the marks inscribed on
the Pilgrim by Angels (or Illumined Ones) at each fresh stage of
his Ascent; Rutherford also constantly in his *Spiritual Letters*
alludes to the "infallible symptoms" or "marks of the elect of
God."   Cf. the fruits of the Spirit, Gal. v. 22.

[2] Isa. xxxiii. 17, xxx. 21.

[3] Mal. iii. 16, 17 ; Dan. xii. 3 ; cf. Luke xxiv. 14, 15.

His sense of scent [1] in this world is correct.
Whether fragrant or ill-smelling,
Instinctively he knows the right.[2]
In desert defiles,
'Mid lions, elephants, tigers, wolves,
Buffaloes or unicorns,
He knows when they conceive,
Whether there will be birth or not,
And if natural or abnormal.
Entering, or coming out from Worship,
Inhales the Incense and knows all.[3]
In his mouth
All turns to sweetness
Like Heaven's dew—
Beautiful, beautiful!
His mouth is clean,[4]
Never admits ill flavours.
What he partakes
Becomes sweet dew.
Should he proclaim a Spiritual Truth,
It is enough to fill the universe.[5]
Freedom it gives to chief of gods and demons—
A great freedom.[6]
If he follows this immortal Scripture,———

---

[1] Cf. Isa. xi. 3 and mg., "Quick of scent-understanding." See p. 253, note 3.

[2] Heb. v. 14, R.V. mg., "perfect"; cf. perfect and complete, lacking nothing.

[3] See p. 161, note 2.

[4] P. 201, note 1.

[5] 2 Tim. ii. 24, 25, iv. 17.

[6] John viii. 32.

His body is most pure
Like crystal,[1]
As a spotless mirror,
Reflecting all things clearly.[2]
But he alone sees clearly,
Others do not see !
All true preachers of the Law
Follow its meaning—
Its eternal meaning,
Not diverging from it.
If we explain ordinary books
And how to rule the world,
How to produce, distribute,
We follow upright laws.
For they are GOD'S Law—
All of them true.
Such men's minds are holy,
What is beneficial they know by intuition.
One should imitate their secret,
To know all truths—the highest, lowest,
      medium.

----

[1] A remarkable passage in the primitive Liturgy of Malabar, used by the St. Thomas Christians, says : " Make us worthy, by Thy love, that in all pureness we may receive the Gift ; and that it may not be unto us for judgment or vengeance, but for love and piety and the remission of sins, and Resurrection from the dead, and Eternal Life ; so that we may all be the fullest witnesses of Thy Glory, and the habitation of a Holy Shrine, that after we have been incorporated into the Body and Blood of Thy Christ with all Thy Saints, we may shine with light, in His ever-glorious and lofty revelation." Cf. Heb. ix. 11.

[2] Cor. iii. 18.

Hearing one verse
Suddenly one understands the Righteousness
        Immeasurable,
And nevermore forgets it !
What this man says
Is the Law of God Eternal.
The man following this Scripture
Dwells in a rare state
Which all creatures
Rejoice in, love and reverence !

CHAPTER XX

Honour the Worthy

Thou who hast received the Highest Power,
The Great Dread Judge (Ta Shih Chih),
Of all I have met
I reverence you the most,
And dare not you his followers despise.
Why ?
Because you all follow the Way of Saints
And will become divine—
Serving GOD only,
And looking from afar on all beings
That they may also turn to GOD,
Worshipping and praising Him.
    If there be any angry

And impure of heart,
Cursing, blaspheming, saying
" These are but ignorant students ! " [1]
And weapons hurl
To harm and injure them.
When listening to them preach with tongues
        of fiery flame,[2]
They all submit and follow,
Preaching all round also [3]
The Law fearlessly.
The Saints they nevermore despise.
Is it strange ?
It is My Body which is thus honoured.[4]
After angering
And despising
For two hundred myriad years
        And never meeting GOD,
Not hearing the Law,
Nor seeing any Preacher,
Dwelling a thousand years in hell,[5]
Suffering immensely
To expiate their sins,
Still—since they no more despise My saints—
After My death,

[1] John ix. 30–35, xvi. 2, 3.
[2] Acts ii. 3–18 ; cf. vii. 54–60, viii. 1, ix. 1–3, xxvi. 10, 11–19,
1 Tim. i. 12, 13, R.V.
[3] Cf. Eph. iii. 1–8 ; Phil. iv. 7, 8.
[4] Matt. xxv. 34–45 ; cf. Eph. i. 22, 23, iii. 10, R.V.
[5] Cf. 1 Pet. iii. 18–20.

If men shall always read, recite,
Explain, make known,
Or copy this Scripture,
Their sins forgiven are.
When they die
And hear this Scripture,
All evil roots are cleared away
Because of the Spirit's magic power and grace
Adding Eternal Life!
Again, if to all men
One publishes this Scripture
And propagates it,
He shall receive Immeasurable Joy
And, gradually acquiring skill,
Shall quickly find the Way of GOD.

   Therefore, those who practise this
   After My Death
   And hear such Doctrine without doubting,
   They should with all their powers
   Preach everywhere [1] this Scripture
   About GOD, age after age.
   Quickly will such find the Way of GOD.

[1] Luke xxiv. 44–52 ; Acts v. 41, 42, viii. 1–4.

Chapter XXI

The Incarnate's Spiritual Power [1]

[Pentecost]

Tongues of fire widely spread [2]
Throughout the world;
In sacred Places,
From Preachers' chairs [3]
Full million years
All creatures trembled,
And with them seraphs, night-goblins,
Kieutape, Asuras,
Kialoulos, Kinnalos, Moheulochias—
Manlike, but non-human—trembled too,[4]
At God's Almighty Power.[5]
Seeing throughout these suffering worlds,
Immeasurable and infinite,
In all holy Places,
In every Preacher's chair,
Illuminated Ones.
In the realm of transmigration
There is a Saviour
Named Sakyamuni [6]

[1] This chapter speaks of God manifesting Himself sometimes as the Messiah, sometimes as the Holy Spirit.

[2] Acts ii. 1–21, x. 44–48.

[3] A lion's throne is a chair of authority.

[4] P. 187, note 2.   [5] Luke vii. 16, R.V., iv. 42, 43.

[6] See p. 190, note 1. Here, however, "Sâkyamuni" seems from the context to mean God manifested in the flesh.

Who taught the Saints
The Scripture of the Highest School.
The Sacred Lotus-Scripture,
Teaching the Way of Saints
Which GOD approves.
Throughout the Universe [1]
This tongue prevails,
Like that of one's own land.
In short,
All the Ways of the GODlike One,[2]
All the power of the GODlike One,
The Secret Treasures [3] of the GODlike,
All the deep things of the GODlike—
Are in this Scripture
Proclaimed and manifested.[4]
Therefore, after My decease,[5]
With all your mind
Study this Scripture,
Explain and copy it;
If you propagate and practise it
Among all nations;
If you study it,

[1] See p. 235, note 2, also p. 236, note 1.

[2] Chinese Buddhists speak of Julai, the Tathaguta, as "God in manifestation," here translated "the Godlike One." See also p. 249.

[3] Luke ix. 31. Cf. also similar terms in the Primitive Liturgies, *e.g.*, "This Mystery of Gladness." See p. 193, note 3; also p. 211, note 1.

[4] Luke ix. 30, 31; 2 Pet. i. 16–18, R.V.

[5] John xiv. 16–19.

Explain, recite it,
If you preach and practise it—
Where'er this Gospel's found,
Be it in a garden,
Or in a sacred forest,
Beneath a sacred tree,
Or in a monastery,
'Mid white-robed choirs,
In temple halls,
Or in a valley,
E'en in a desert place,
Where'er it be
Build there a Shrine (pagoda) for worship.
Why ?
Because such are sacred colleges
Where the Illumined
Received the highest Truth.
All Illumined ones thus
Preach the Law ;
All the Enlightened thus
Proclaim Eternal Life [1]
To rejoice the hearts of men.
Now is made manifest
The Infinite power Divine,
The merit of the One—
Immeasurable, Unlimited,
Like space, limitless.
Those who follow this Scripture

[1] See p. 147, note 2 ; 1 John i. 2.

Have already seen Me,
And beheld the God of many Treasures,[1]
And the members of My Broken Body.[2]
They see Me, too, this day
Training many followers.
Those who follow this Scripture
Receive Me and My Broken Body.
The Dead yet Living GOD OF ALL GRACE
And the Delivered all rejoice.
The present Saints,
The past and future Saints,
Are seen and reverenced,
And made glad.
Such men are in GOD'S way
Assuredly, without a doubt.

CHAPTER XXII

Be One

Rising in His Throne
He exhorted, saying
You who are one-minded [3]
In the spreading of this Law,

[1] Cf. Col. i. 19, ii. 10, bodily, lit. in a bodily form ; 1 Pet. v. 10 ; John i. 16. "This God is one who divides Himself and is the Mystery in the Lotus Scripture" (Eitel). John i. 14 ; 1 Cor. xi. 24–26. See also p. 254.

[2] Luke xxiv. 30–35 ; 1 Cor. xii. 27, 28. Cf. John xiv. 9, xiii. 20.

[3] John xvii. 21–26.

Extend it widely,

So that all creatures

Everywhere may hear it.[1]

　There is great Mercy,

　Without grudging,

　And without fear.

　I manifest GOD,

　The greatest Benefactor

　Of all living creatures.

　Those who believe My words

　Should constantly this Scripture preach;

　In me they have abundance

　Of instruction, and great joy.[2]

To be grateful

For all the grace of the Illumined,

E'en sacrificing their bodies.[3]

With deepest reverence should they overflow,[4]

With body prostrate, and with bowèd head,

With folded palms to GOD-ward turned.[5]

[1] Luke xxiv. 44–47.

[2] John x. 10, Life; viii. 12, Light; xiv. 25, 26, xvi. 12–14, Teaching; xv. 11, xvii. 13, Joy; xiv. 27, Peace.

[3] Rom. xii. 1; Eph. v. 1, 2; Rev. xii. 11; cf. "jeopardised" in Judg. v. 18, R.V.; 1 Chron. xi. 17–19.

[4] "Adoration is no mere prostration of the body; it is a prostration of the soul," said Canon Liddon.

[5] So also the Creation tablet of Babylonia, as translated by Professor Delitzsch :—

　　"Towards the God, thou shouldest be of pure heart,
　　That is dearest to the Deity.　Prayers, supplications,
　　Prostrations of face, thou shouldest offer Him early
　　Every morning.　Mercy becomes the fear of God;
　　Sacrifice enhances life; prayer absolves from sin."

All heard a Voice,
Like the command of GOD :——
"Let all obey." [1]
Hearing these words Divine,
All greatly rejoiced.

CHAPTER XXIII

The Physician

Now all men
Rejoiced to see Disciples
Gladly practising austerities
In the broad noon of spiritual virtue,
Growing thus in grace [2]
With their whole mind seeking GOD,
That they might better learn
The virtue of this Scripture,
Yet this equals not the service of one's life.[3]
This sure growth in grace
Is called " the true Way "
Of worshipping the GODlike One.
'Tis the highest offering,——

And in the Prayer of Intense Adoration in the Divine Liturgy of
St. Mark which was used daily at Alexandria in the fourth century,
and has its place in all Oriental Liturgies : " We have bowed the
neck of our souls and bodies signifying the outward appearance of
service."

[1] Matt. xvii. 5 ; Heb. i. 6. [2] 1 Pet. iii. 18.
[3] Rom. xii. 1 ; 1 Cor. xv. 58.

Amongst all gifts—

Most honourable, and highest.

This, therefore, is the Way to reverence

All the Godlike

Who diligently grow in grace,

Yielding their precious lives.

Then upon the seashore

In honour they raise a funeral pyre—

Ignite it ; after being burned,

Collect the sacred Ashes

In eighty-four thousand urns [1]

To erect eighty-four thousand Shrines (pagodas) [2]
  (stupas),

High as the Heavens,

With glorious towers,

With banners flying,

And precious bells.

Thus they return to Heaven with their
  disciples,

Happy and wise, having " attained perfection." [3]

Filled with all precious things of the universe,

They make offering unto GOD,

[1] See p. 247.

[2] The Pagoda is essentially a sepulchral monument ; the Chinese and Japanese counterpart of the Indian stupa. Cf. Rev. vi. 9–11.

[3] Another term derived from the ancient Mysteries. See p. 153, note 2 ; p. 162, note 5 ; p. 251, note, 1. Cf. Phil. iii. 12–15, mg. R.V., "full grown," where it is used with other Mystery-terms, "Press on" and "Lay hold."

Note also that "Perfection" is a key-word in the Epistle to the Hebrews ii. 10, v. 9, vi. 1 (mg. "full grown") with those other

To the Great Saints,
To the Doctors of the Buddhist Law,
And to the devout (Arhats) of every school,
But the virtue offered equals not
That of following, practising
One four-lined verse [1] of this Pure Doctrine,
For the reward will be far greater,
With the King in Glory dwelling.
Of all streams and rivers,
Of all waters,
The sea is greatest,
As GOD is chief in the spirit-world.
So is this Scripture chief
Among all Scriptures.
It can save all living creatures,
It can lead all living creatures,
To be rid of every trouble.
This Scripture can immensely benefit
All living creatures,
Fulfilling their desires—
As a place of coolness
Quenching all kinds of thirst,
It resembles the frozen finding fire,

Mystery-terms "Enlightened," "Tasted," "Made Partakers."
Again, Heb. vii. 19, where it is used in connection with the Mystery-
terms "A Better Hope" and "Draw nigh" (vv. 19, 25) ; also vii.
28, "A Son perfected for evermore" ; Heb. ix. 11, x. 1, 14, and
cf. vv. 32, 33, "Enlightened, becoming partakers"—"perfected
for ever" ; also xii. 2, R.V., "Jesus the Author and Perfecter of
our Faith."

[1] See pp. 131, 241, note.

The naked finding clothes,
Or merchants finding trade;
Like babes who find the mother's breast,
A man who at a ferry finds a boat,
Or sick ones finding health,
Or blind eyes finding light,
Like beggars finding wealth,
As rebels find a chief,
As bridegroom finds his bride,
As light from which the darkness flees—
So is this Lotus Scripture,
Able to lead all creatures
Out of all troubles,
All sickness, every pain,
And rid them of all chains of life, or death.
If one hears the Living Scripture
If one copies it,
Or makes others copy it,
The reward
Is Divine wisdom
Whose value
Is limitless,
For never shall any
As suffering women [1] be re-born.

[1] Gal. iii. 28. Describing the terrific tortures to which the martyrs were subjected, Eusebius, writing from Cæsarea, *cir.* A.D. 303–313, says: "The females also, no less than the men, were strengthened by the Doctrine of the Divine Word, so that some endured the same trials as the men and bore away the same prizes of excellence."

Thinking o'er this Scripture,
And revealing it to others,
The reward is boundless, inexhaustible !
Fire cannot burn it,
Nor water wash away
Your Blessings.
A thousand Illumiued Ones say
That they can ne'er exhausted be
Already you can rush through Devils' ranks
Destroying armies of Death [1]
And remaining enemies
Annihilating them all.
After My Death and Deliverance,
Five hundred years later,[2]
'Twill be widely spread [3]

[1] When arraigned before the Emperor Trajan at Rome, St. Ignatius of Antioch said : " I go my way to Him ; He is the Bread of Immortality, and the Draught of Eternal Life, and I am wholly His—therefore I despise thy tortures and reject the honours. Let loose thy beasts that I may become pure bread." When Trajan heard these things he was greatly astonished (cf. p. 211, note 1). In the same spirit the Chinese Pilgrim Hiouen Tsang (who in the seventh century travelled to India " to recover the Law which was to be a Guide to all men and the means of their salvation ") said : " I know that the King in spite of his power has no power over my mind and my will " ; and again, " Robbers are men, and at present, when I am going to adore the Shadow of Buddha, even though the roads were full of wild beasts I should walk on without fear."—Max Müller, *Chips*, vol. i. pp. 265, 268.

[2] Note the reference to the prophesy of p. 131.

[3] The Lotus Scripture and the Doctrine of the Three Precious Ones was translated into Chinese first by Dharmaraksha, A.D. 266–313 or 317, when he died seventy-seven years old. It came to N. Korea A.D. 372, to S. Korea 384, and to Japan A.D. 552.

Throughout strange lands.[1]

It cannot be destroyed

By devils,[2] or their followers,

Dragons or night ogres,

Or any monstrous demons.

'Tis worthy to be preserved

Amongst a King's treasures.

You should use your magic powers

To preserve this Scripture.

[1] This is historically true only of the Gospel of Jesus Christ; Rev. xiv. 6. Clement of Rome, the contemporary of St. Paul, said that the Apostle "travelled to the furthest limits of the West"; and in A.D. 193 Tertullian in N. Africa wrote, "In whom else have all nations believed, but in Christ? Parthians, Medes, Elamites, all the coasts of Spain, the various nations of Gaul and the parts inaccessible to the Romans" (*i.e.* the highlands of Britain behind Hadrian's Great Wall) "are now accessible to Christ." The martyrdoms at Lyons in Gaul took place in A.D. 177; those at Carthage in Africa 202; St. Albans in Britain 286, where there were numerous others (286–292) between Amiens and Marseilles. Again, 303–313, "an innumerable multitude of martyrs from Libya and through all Egypt, Syria, round as far as the region of Illyricum," says Eusebius. Arnobius in the third century counted the Seres or Chinese amongst the nations who had received the Gospel. St. Jerome (*d.* 420), speaking of the Divine Word, the Son of God, being everywhere present in His fulness in all places, he adds, "with Thomas in India, with Peter at Rome, with Paul in Illyrica." Refer also to p. 227, note 1 : "Throughout the Universe this tongue prevails," etc. When the Japanese Emperor received the Image of Shakya Butsu and the Inner Doctrine of the Greater Way in 552, the Nihongi chronicler records that he said, "The countenance of this Buddha is of a severe dignity such as we have never at all seen before, ought it to be worshipped or not?," and the reply was, "All the Western frontier lands without exception do it worship : Shall Akitsu Yamato alone refuse to do so?"—Aston's *Nihongi*, ii. pp. 65, 66.

[2] Rom. viii. 31, especially Rev. xii. 3–17.

Why ?
Because 'tis healing for all nations,[1]
The sick man's Medicine.
If one hear this Scripture,
His sickness ends.
The patient grows not old, nor dies.
All creatures are delivered from
The sea of trouble, old age, sickness—even
    death.

CHAPTER XXIV

Wonderful News

[Transfiguration ?]

The flesh and hair shine,
E'en the forehead shines
And whitened hairs shed light.[2]
It is because all virtue
Was planted long ago.
The body is immovable,
Having entered into ecstasy.
Extraordinary virtue [3] brightly burns
And shines with glory,
The form is quite complete,
Strong like the Creator [4]
All filial,

[1] Rev. xxii. 1, 2.
[2] Matt. xvii. 2–5 ; Mark ix. 3 ; Luke ix. 29.
[3] Luke v. 15, 17, 26, ix. 19 ; Matt. ix. 33.
[4] Rev. i. 14–16 ; Dan. vii. 9 ; 2 Pet. i. 16–18, R.V.

Worships no Shamans,
Seeing evil, is grieved at heart,
Although unmoved by passion,
Peaceful, with few troubles,
Able to endure.[1]
With eighty-four thousand priests [2]
Visited all the hells,[3]
Lived 'mid hungry ghosts and animals,[4]
Endured all kinds of difficulty.
Thus enabled all to save,
Even in royal palaces.
Became a woman
That she might preach this Scripture,
To plant the Seed of Goodness
And manifest itself in all
Human existence.
Then once again returned
To her first state of soul in GOD,[5]
Rejoicing in the joy this Scripture gives.

[1] Heb. xi. 27 ; Jas. i. 12, v. 11, R.V.
[2] See p. 247.
[3] 1 Pet. iii. 18, 19.
[4] Mark i. 13, R.V. The Japanese Buddhists of the Shinshu Hongwangi, or sect of the True Original Vow, say, " that Amida is God, but to save men He suffered and died, and went through the Forty-eight Hells for them."
[5] John viii. 23, xiii. 1–3, xvi. 27, 28, xvii. 8.

CHAPTER XXV

Kwanyin—[The Universal Hearer of Prayer] [1]

[See General Introduction, vi. p. 16, for fuller translation than this Essence.]

The Incomprehensible (Holy Spirit),
She whom no evil spirit's eyes can see—
Much less harm—
Baffles them all,
Granting deliverance.
The wondrous power of GOD
Is awe-inspiring, like this :—
Should a woman desire a son,
And reverently worship
Holy Kwanyin,[2]
She will obtain a blessing—
An intelligent son.

[1] Like the Holy Spirit who is the Hearer of Prayer ; cf. Rom. viii. ; 1 Kings viii. 27–52 ; Ps. cvii. ; Faber's Hymn, "When the weary, seeking rest," etc.

[2] Kwanyin (the Indian "Avalo-kitesvara," Japanese "Kwanon") is "the Listening Goddess" whom prayer will instantly cause to appear anywhere by land or sea. She has appeared in thirty-three bodies or forms (classes of society), wishing to succour each class of human beings as best suited to his special spiritual needs. "Her Mercy is higher than the mountains, deeper than the torrent-riven valleys." Cf. Mark xvi. 16, "After this He appeared unto them in another form" ; also Ex. ii. 23, 24, iii. 7 ; Ps. xxxii. 13 ; Deut. xxxiii. 27, "the God of old time" (Variorum), and especially Luke i. 48 ; John ix. 34, 35.

Should she desire a daughter,
She brings forth a virtuous one,
A beauteous daughter,
Rooted deep in virtue,
By all respected,
Joy without alloy,
Immeasurable,—infinite
Are these blessings.
In three and thirty forms
Herself, she manifested,
Vowed a great vow, deep like the sea,
A vow of holiness.   Trusting in her power
A fiery furnace becomes a cooling lake of water,[1]
Waves cannot drown;
Through her kindliness of heart
Shivered is sword of executioner.
Accursed poisonous herbs [2]
May life endanger, but—
Think upon the Lotus Law
And you will then be healed.
'Mid thunder-clouds and lightning,
Hailstones and floods of rain,
Look up to Kwanyin.
These all shall vanish.
Kwanyin's wondrous knowledge
Can save a world of sorrow.[3]
'Tis mercy upon mercy—
Purest Light !

[1] Cf. *ante*, p. 177, note 4.   [2] Mark xvi. 17, 18.   [3] Cf. Acts v. 18–20.

Wisdom's Sun dispels the darkness,
Subdues calamities of wind and fire ;
Shines brightly o'er the world ;
Is full of goodness,
Beams kindly on all creatures.
Blessings like the sea abound,
Therefore revere her.
Heaven's own dew and rain will fall,
Extinguishing flames of trouble,
And exorcising feelings of revenge.
In your hearts harbour no doubt,
But trust in holy Kwanyin,
In all trouble, danger, even death—
Then you have One on whom to lean !

CHAPTER XXVI

Toloni (calling Demons to aid by Magic)

If one doth follow
This Lotus Gospel,
Even one four-lined verse,[1]
Read, recite, explain it,
Preach and practise it—
His reward is very great.
An—ur Man—ur, etc. (spells),
If one destroys

[1] Pp. 131, 233.

16

Such Spiritual Guides,
It will be like destroying
The Illuminated.
The arch-Prince Pisamen,[1]
Who protects the world,
Pities all creatures,
And He will protect these Spiritual Guides.
Whoever follows this Scripture,
For one hundred yeusheun [2]
No evil shall befall him.
The Angels who rule the nations [3]
Will then have female Locha,
One called " Lan Po,"
The second " Pe Kanko,"
The third " Crooked Teeth,"
The fourth " Flower Teeth,"
The fifth " Black Teeth,"
The sixth " Hairy,"
The seventh " Insatiable,"
The eighth " Jewel Bearer,"
The ninth " Hao Ti,"
The tenth " Sucker of all vitals "—
These ten female Lochas,
With demons and their mothers
And their children—
All their progeny,—

[1] Pisamen—Vaisramana, King of Yakcha, a Beelzebub converted
by Sakyamuni, who now protects the Law.

[2] One yeusheun—5½ English miles.

[3] Cf. Dan. x. 13, 20, 21, xii. 1.

Gathered in GOD's Presence,
With one voice they thus addressed Him:
" World-honoured One !
We, too, desire to guard
Those who study and follow
The Lotus Scripture,
To deliver them from all
Feebleness and trouble.
Should they seek deceitfully
To criticise the Spiritual Guides,
Making things hard for them—
Or have caused them fever,
Whether for one day or two,
Three days or four, e'en seven days
They suffer constant fever—
May this fall upon our heads
Rather than on the Spiritual Guides.
If, disobeying us,
They should annoy the Guides,
Then let their head be split in seven,
Like the branches of the banyan tree.
Their crime is great as parricide,
Boiled should they be in oil.
Priest-detractors resemble those
Who cheat with weights and measures,
And should likewise be severely punished."

CHAPTER XXVII

Kwanyin's Royal Human Parents

A pure Princess
With two folded palms
Thus addressed her Mother-queen,
" I pitying my father
Show these signs—
Above the body there is water,[1]
Below the body there is fire.
Again, below there comes forth water
And above comes forth fire.
For my father's weal,
We worshipped GOD,
Left home to practise the Good Law.
Mother, permit me
To become a nun (Shaman).
The Illumined are not easily met,
I desire to learn and follow them.
Truly, beloved parents,
The Illumined Ones are rarely met
Like the Yeu-hing-po-lo-hwa.[2]
We are like one-eyed turtles
Seeking refuge in a floating wood.
We change our evil hearts

---

[1] Matt. iii. 11 ; John iii. 5.
[2] This is a fig tree that flowers only once in three thousand years.

In order peace to find
In the Faith of the Illumined
And see the One world-honoured God.
The learned in the fundamentals
Of civilisation, say
They lead to God,
And to the discovery
Of highest Wisdom.
Pitying the wrong doctrines of the world,
We guide to the True Knowledge.
The Godlike Way
Can fully be attained,
Though beyond thought
Its merits are,
Giving instruction to its learners,
Bestowing rest and speedy goodness.
From this day forth we
Will not follow our own wills,
Neither pursue wild ways,
Nor pride, nor anger cherish,
Filled with all seeds of sins,
But straight will go unto the root of Good,
And win what passes all imagining,
The greatest harvest!"

CHAPTER XXVIII

Command to Saint Universal Good (Pu Hien)

GOD said to Pu Hien—
" If good men and virtuous women
Would use the four means of grace
After the GODlike One's Decease,
They should seek the Living Scripture—

    1. Win all the Illumined to their side.

    2. Seek the root of all Goodness—

    3. Attend the gatherings of the Upright— [1]

    4. Vow to save all living beings.

You good men, virtuous women,
If you follow these four means of grace
After the GODlike One's Decease,
Then you certainly will find this Scripture."
Then Pu Hien
Answered GOD, saying—
" World-honoured One,
Five hundred years hence,
Amidst this evil world
There will be those who follow this Scripture—
Upholding such men,
I shall rid them of perplexities
And bid them rest in peace,—
Nor let those who seek their own
And those who trouble men

[1] Cf. Heb. x. 24, 25, xii. 14, 15, xiii. 2–7, 15–17.

Succeed.
If such ones forget the Verses
Of the Living Scripture,
I will teach them [1]
To read, recite it,
And receive its full benefits.
No evil men
Can injure them,
And they shall not
By women be allured.
I shall Myself
Protect these men."

    Be the Living Scripture [2]
    Practised by the uncivilised Nations [3]
    And followed by them—
    They should have this thought,
    All is Pu Hien's
    Wondrous spiritual power,[4]
    By all the Godlike ones ordainèd,
With hands upon their heads,[5]
Eighty-four thousand [6] heavenly Angels,
With all kinds of music— [7]
Come forth to meet them—

---

[1] " Bring all things to your remembrance," John xiv. 26, xvi. 13–15.

[2] 2 Cor. iii. 2, 3.   [3] Acts xxi. 19, xxii. 21.

[4] 2 Cor. xii. 9, 10 ; Eph. vi. 10, mg. R.V.

[5] Acts vi. 6, xiii. 3 ; 2 Tim. i. 6. The Nestorian Christian missionaries had "the Ordination of the Five Talents."

[6] See "84,000," p. 106. Cf. the "144,000" of Rev. vii. 4, 9.

[7] Luke xv. 7, 25.

Such ones
Wear sevenfold crowns.[1]
When these die
Thousands of Illumined ones [2] receive him,
He has no fear
Of sinking to an evil place.[3]
World-honoured One—
I shall with powers miraculous
Uphold this Scripture
Among the Nations
After My Death,
And make it widely known,
So that it shall never cease to lead
Multitudes of creatures
To dwell in peace, and joy, and blessing.
If any study it
And its true meaning—
Practise and copy
This Living Scripture—
You should know that this One
Has seen GOD (Sakyamuni),[4]
As though he heard from His own lips
This Scripture.
You should know that this man
Respects GOD (Sakyamuni),
You should know that this one

---

[1] 2 Tim. iv. 8.
[2] 1 Thess. iv. 16, 17.   [3] Luke xvi. 22.
[4] See p. 189, note 4 ; p. 226, note 6.

Is praised by GOD as "faithful."[1]
You should know that
He is GOD'S (Sakyamuni) fore-ordainèd Man!
You should recognise that this Man is
Clothed with
GOD's Mantle.[2]
Such men covet not this world—
Nor follow its erroneous teachings;
In all their writings
One straight course pursue
And upright aim,[3]
Have powers of goodness,
Possessing few desires, are satisfied.[4]
Such men shall soon
Be asked by others to instruct.
They covet not
Fine clothes, nor ease,[5]
Nor dainties of the Feast.
What they desire is no vain show,
Nor do they seek in this life to gain reward.
To such rewards be ever blind,

[1] "Faithful," Matt. xxv. 21–23. It is a term used in the "Book of the Dead," *e.g.* "Faithful to the Great God;—true of voice like Osiris," *i.e.* "perfectly in tune," as the reason for Justification in the great "Judgment of Account of Words" in the Vermilion Hall (Maspero). See p. 256, note 4.

[2] 1 Kings xix. 19. Cf. Gal. iii. 27, 28, R.V., "As many of you were baptized into Christ did put on Christ." See *ante*, p. 185, note 2.

[3] Phil. iii. 13; 2 Cor. vi. 10.

[4] Phil. iv. 8, R.V., "learned the secret"; lit. been initiated.

[5] Matt. iii. 4.

If you honour praise-seekers—
Honour them in this world.
But if, again, you see a follower
Of this Scripture,
Criticising its shortcomings,[1]
Imaginary or real,
That man in this life
Has got the leprosy !

EPILOGUE

GOOD WILL TO MEN

The Gospel of Holy Pu Hien (Universal Good)

[The Text of the Chinese Essence is taken from selected
passages in Pu Hien Hing Fa King's Nanjio's Catalogue, No.
394, Trans.]

Three months hence
I shall pass away.
Though troubles have not ceased,
And character be still imperfect,
Yet shall I of evil roots be rid,
And end my sin.
Not in ecstasy,[2]

---

[1] Acts xix. 8, 9.

[2] This is a mark or characteristic of a saint. When a holy
man, such as a Buddhist Abbot, is about to die, he is raised
into a sitting posture, his disciples gathered round, and with a
loud voice, gathering up all his failing strength, the dying saint

But by chanting this Scripture
With mind bent on practising it.
And all my thoughts collected
Within the Great Religion,
I feel lost in infinite space ;
Hearing infinite sounds,
Surrounded with infinite forms,
All in a divine chorus
Praising the Great Religion,
The One True Way,
Praising the Great Gospel,
Reciting the Great Gospel,
Thinking of the Great Gospel,
Studying the Great Gospel fruits ;
Those reverently worshipping,
And " laying hold " [1] of it,
Behold all men

chants aloud this Lotus Sutra or some poetry which he himself
composed. It will be remembered that our Lord when upon the
Cross refused the stupefying draught, the anodyne offered to Him
by a kindly soldier who heard His cry (Mark xv. 23 ; Matt. xxvii.
34). His loud expiring cry convinced the Centurion, who was
watching His dying agonies, that He was a Son of God, because
" He so gave up the ghost " (Mark xv. 34–39). A Buddhist priest
first called my attention to the fact that this was the death of a
Bodhisattva. He had been profoundly impressed by that cry,
which was of Victory over Death—that of a Conqueror who had
destroyed the sting of Death, brought Immortality to light, and
opened the Gates of the Kingdom of Heaven to all believers.

[1] " Lay hold "—" Hold fast " (expressions much used in the Epistle
to the Hebrews and the Revelation) are terms derived straight from
the Mystery-teachings of the Ancient Wisdom. See *ante*, p. 151,
note 2 ; p. 161, note 2 ; p. 232, note 3 ; also p. 209, note 1.

As God sees them,

And all living creatures

As parents view their children.

Thinking of the Great Religion,

Night and day unceasingly,

I heard Pu Hien preaching

On its depth of meaning

So as to "hold it fast"[1] without forget-
fulness.[2]

With upright heart and upright aim,

Gradually one comes to see,

By means of this Great Teaching,[3]

The Great Instructor (Kwanyin, Holy
Spirit ?).

And through this Great Instructor's power

To see all the Illumined,

Waking or sleeping,

Never leave their side,[4]

And e'en in dreams[5] should see

The seven Illumined ancient patriarchs (?).[6]

When dark crimes

.And all sins

[1] See note 1 on p. 251.

[2] Heb. xii. 5 ; 2 Pet. i. 9 ; Gal. iv. 3, 9, R.V.

[3] Mark i. 27, R.V., " What is this ? A New Teaching ! with
authority He commandeth even the unclean spirits and they obey
Him."

[4] See pp. 155, 206, note 2 ; 2 Kings vi. 14–16 ; Josh. v. 13–
15, etc.

[5] Job xxxiii. 15. See p. 203, note 4.

[6] Cf. the Seven Rishis of the Veda, also Seven Spirits before
God's throne, Rev. i.

Were revealed before the World-honoured
    Ones—
Confession was made,
Words gradually were heard
Above those of this world—[1]
Gradually the eye sees things
Beyond this world:[2]
By degrees the nose smells[3]
Incense not of earth—
Body and soul are filled with joy—
Because sin is no more.[4]
In former lives we,
By means of the Great School,
Acquired this life's
Pure, upright knowledge.
These Scriptures of the New School
Are the treasures of all the Illumined,
Are the eyes of the Illumined
In all three Realms of the Universe,
Past, Present, and to come,
Appearing as Incarnate Ones
As the Godlike Ones,—
Following these Scriptures,

[1] Isa. xxx. 20, 21, note clairvoyance and clairaudience, 2 Cor.
xii. 1–3.

[2] Cf. 2 Cor. iv. 16–18; Heb. xi. 27. "Grant me then insight
into Thy Mysteries" was the Psalmist's prayer, Ps. lxxiii. 17
(Wellhausen's rendering).

[3] Isa. xi. 2, 3, lit. "quick of scent," *i.e.* understanding, mg.
Cf. Heb. v. 11–14; 1 Tim. iv. 6, 7; 1 John v. 1–3.   See p. 220.

[4] Heb. ix. 24–26 R.V., 28.

Men become divine,
And do the works of GOD.[1]
Follow the Great School,
Let not its spiritual seed fail ;
Follow the Great School
With all its wondrous principles.
Then you shall see all the Illumined
And the sunshine of their face [2]
Reflected in their followers' hearts,
Behold the PRESENCE REAL,[3]
Clearly, distinctly !
Study GOD,
Study His Laws,
Study the students of these Laws,
Their discipline, their charity,
Their Heaven.
Beauty blinds your eyes,[4]
Enslaves you to its pleasure.
By rightly thinking of this Great School,
Never forgetting it
To all eternity,
You will not into evil fall.
Whoever has this mind
Possesses the right mind.

[1] John vii. 31, ix. 32, xiv. 12, xv. 24 ; Acts xxvi. 16–18.
[2] "The Hidden Faces which guard the Road" ; cf. Ps. xxxiv. 5,
"They looked unto Him, and their faces were made radiant,"
R.V.
[3] See chap. xxi. p. 95 ; John xiii. 35, xvii. 21–23 ; cf.
1 John i. 2, "The Life was manifested."
[4] Prov. xxxi. 30.

Should you deviate
You become a pervert,
But the Church of the GOD OF ALL GRACE
    endures ever,[1]
Can preach the great Law
And shower its life-giving rain
To set aright the ignorant.[2]
All those who listen
Constantly to bad words
Produce all kinds of strange ideas
By inquiring in the wrong way.[3]
Such deserve to sink into the Way of the
    wicked,[4]
Where they see nothing but evil,
Where this Scripture ne'er is heard.
The Scripture Expansions (Fang Têng)[5]
Have Love and Mercy for their theme.
The words which they repeat

[1] See chap. xxi. p. 95.

[2] John xii. 8, xvii. 11 ; 1 Tim iii. 15.

[3] 1 Tim. vi. 3-5, R.V. ; 2 Pet. ii. 1, 2 ; 2 Tim. ii. 15-18,
R.V.

[4] Iranæus in the second century wrote : "There are those who
have heard Polycarp tell how John, the disciple of the Lord, when
he went to take a bath at Ephesus, saw Cerinthus (the famous
heretical teacher) within, and rushed away from the room without
bathing, with the words 'Let us flee lest the room should fall in,
for Cerinthus the enemy of the Truth is within.'" Cited by
Eusebius.

[5] These Fang Têng Scriptures (Vaipulya) are amplified and
diffused editions first introduced into China A.D. 266 (Eitel) ; first
translated into Chinese by Dharmaraksha (Nanjio's Catalogue, p.
391).

Are of the world of the Illumined,
The principles of the Great School—
Are True Realities beneath all forms.

All the Illumined and the Godlike
   Ones
Are your Loving Father's.[1]
All evil thoughts come from the tongue,[2]
Stopping Truth's progress,
From the tongue,
Therefore, because of evil language,
Man falleth into hell.

It also uses loving speech
Promoting good feeling,
In the midst of ill,
Its object never fails.

Sakyamuni [3]
Who is the chief God Vairochana,[4]
Who pervades all space,
Where He dwells is called
The Calm, Eternal Light.
An endless chain,
A boundless ocean,
Purposeful seeming purposeless,

[1] Cf. 2 Cor. iv. 14, 15, R.V.

[2] The connection with St. James' Epistle is clear. He was the brother of the Lord Jesus Christ. See iii. 2–12.

[3] See *ante*, p. 193, note 3. Sakyamuni seems to be used to represent the human and the divine.

[4] Vairochana (Sanscrit Jap. Dainichi) is the Everywhere Present Sun. The Dainichi Scripture or "Great Sun classic" was brought to China at a very early date.

Baffling thought.
   What is sin ?
   What happiness ?
   The true soul is free,
   Unmoved by rewards or punishments.
   The great repentance,
   The great and glorious at-one-ment (?),[1]
   The sinless atonement (?),
   This transcends all human thought.
These Scripture Expansions (Vaipulya)
Are the eyes of all the Illumined.
They, on this account,
Possess five eyes (the five Wisdom Command-
     ments ?),
Have three forms (Trinity ?),[2]
From the Expansions arise
Great spiritual evidence—
The evidence of Everlasting Life.
In this Eternal sea
Producing three Orders (Divinity, Laws and
     the Teachers of these ?)
Divinely pure—
These three Orders [3]

---

[1] *Ante*, p. 249, note 1, "attunement." The sense in which the word is used by Shakespeare and John Bunyan—
     "Then Heaven tries the earth
       If it be in tune " ;
and again, "God always begins with the bass when He means to set the soul in tune for Himself—for the bass is the keynote of all music."—*Pilgrim's Progress*.

[2] Or body, soul, and spirit.   [3] Matt. xxviii. 19.

17

Afford realms of Joy for God and men.
Reverence the Highest.
Only chant the Great School (Mahayana),
Study the chief righteousness,
And diligently cultivate mercy.
If you desire always to dwell
In the Eternal City,
In joy and peace,
Immeasurable goodness
From this truth flows.
All waves of difficulty
Arise from false ideas.
If you desire repentance,
Sit down, consider your true state ;
Then all your sins shall vanish
As hoar-frost melts before the Rising Sun.

   If any read, recite, and propagate
   The Expansions,
   And night and day reverence
   The Illumined Saints,
   Those who pursue this Law
   Obey GOD's Laws
   And celebrate their uses,
   Reciting the Scriptures of the Great School,
   They meditate upon the highest righteous-
      ness—
   Most deep, eternal Law.
   In the time it takes to snap one's fingers,
   One is released from sins of millions ages.

These are called " Perfect Disciples,"
Who need no transmigration to obtain perfect
    Karma.
Naturally they become perfect.
The World-honoured Ones
Always abide in the world.[1]
On account of our evil habits,
Though we believe the Expansions,
We cannot see GOD to-day.
If, following the Expansions,
One be willing life to lose,
Though one should sink into Purgatory
And suffer countless torments—
If he curses not
The piety of Saints
But turns to GOD,
And to the Law,
And to the Teachers of GOD'S Laws,
Whether at home or in a monastery,
They need no priests,
Nor any teachers,
Nor speak of Karma
To obtain the Scriptural Salvation [2]
Of the Great School.
For half the work is done already,
With every thought
Quickly repenting of their sins
Once and for ever.

[1] Matt. xxviii. 20.   [2] Heb. vii. 25.

Those who do ill themselves
And declare GOD's Law is ill,
And write that all such evils
As stealing and licentiousness
Are not shameful—
Nor any sins,[1]
Blaspheming the Scriptures of Salvation,
And abounding in all ill—
All great ill-doers
Will have their recompense with wicked souls
In fearful storms,
And must fall into lowest hell.

    Those who repent and pray,
      If only they are earnest in their heart—
      Do not blaspheme the Precious Order
        Three;[2]
      Nor hinder men becoming Teachers of
        Divine Law,
      Commit no ill against Lay Teachers,
      But contribute to and respect
      The followers of the Great School.
      You must also reverence
      And be filial to your parents,
      Respect your teachers and your elders;

[1] See also p. 193, note 3 ; p. 213 ; p. 217, note 1 ; p. 235, note 2 ; p. 256, note 3.

[2] The Three Precious Ones are—1, God ; 2, God's Laws throughout the Universe ; 3, those who teach and apply them for the good of all men, *i.e.* the Priesthood. Or God in Three Persons (Amida, Dai Seishi, Kwannon as in Japan. In China, Omito Fu, Ta Shih Chih, and Kwanyin), p. 12.

With upright Law the nation rule,
With all your might
Avoid destroying the people;[1]
Firmly believe in Eternal recompense
And that whole-heartedly.
Know too that GOD is not dead,
Therefore—be not led astray !

[1] "Put an end to war" occurs in the Primitive Liturgy of St. James, the Lord's brother. "Deliver, O Lord, this city and every city and country from . . . sword, civil war . . . Quiet the schisms of the Churches, quench the boasting of the nations . . . by the power of the Holy Spirit, etc., that of St. Basil the Great."

VI

THE GREAT PHYSICIAN'S TWELVE
DESIRES (VOWS)

NOTE

THE first Buddhist temple in or around Nara in Japan was built by Koreans, at the invitation of the Japanese rulers in the sixth century of the Christian era.

One of the most remarkable sights I have seen in Japan is a temple at Horiyuji, near Nara, to the Great Physician (Yakushi they call him). It is filled with innumerable votive offerings, to show that the sick were healed by prayers to him. The zeal of modern Christian scientists is far more than eclipsed by this wonderful record of fifteen centuries there.

By bringing the highest ideals of the East and the West together for comparison, it is hoped that special attention should be called to this rather than to the failings and low practices of either East or West.

The Scripture which describes this Great Physician has one very striking passage on his twelve Vows or Purpose in coming to the world. These twelve Vows I translate below :—

1. I come from Heaven with the highest wisdom to shine on infinite innumerable worlds accompanied by thirty-two great angels, different forms of Kwanyin (see p. 16), and glorious legions, it will be for the purpose of delivering all beings, to be godlike like myself.

2. I come with my body within and without pure as crystal, without a flaw, with great light and profound virtue living in peace with a glory surpassing that of sun and moon, it will be to enlighten all who are living in darkness.

3. I come again with wisdom bringing infinite knowledge and goodness so that no living creature may suffer from any want but have all they need.

4. I come in order that those who are in evil ways may find peace in the way of wisdom, and in order that those who only know the old Buddhism, may know the new Buddhism.

5. I come in order that the multitudes who study religion may discover the perfect way, and if they have erred on hearing my name may be delivered from hell, and also attain to holiness.

6. I come so that all beings who are cripples, ugly and foolish, blind, deaf and dumb, hunchback, leprous and mad, and all sorts of suffering, on

hearing my name may be healed of all their diseases.

7. I come so that the incurables, the homeless, those without doctors or medicine, without friends or relatives, the poor and the sorrowful, on hearing my name shall be delivered from all their troubles and live in peace of mind and body, have their families flourish in abundance and attain the highest wisdom.

8. I come so that women driven by all sorts of trials to hate their lives, and no longer desire to be women, on hearing my name may be changed to men, and attain the highest wisdom.

9. I come so that those who are in the bonds of evil spirits, or of heresies fallen into all sorts of evil, on hearing my name may be led to right knowledge, and gradually practise goodness and attain to the highest wisdom.

10. I come so that those who have fallen to the clutches of the law, are bound and beaten and imprisoned, or are about to be executed or have endless calamities, insults, sorrows burning both body and soul, on hearing my name may secure my grace and power, and be delivered from all their sorrows.

11. I come so that those driven by hunger and thirst to do wrong, on hearing my name shall be fed and satisfied with wisdom and find perfect rest.

12. I come so that all the poor and naked, and

those suffering from heat and cold, and divers flies
and secret creepers night and day, on hearing my
name may turn to practise religion, according to
their bent, will receive the garments of highest
wisdom, glorious treasures and best music, and be
fully satisfied with all.

VII

THE CREED OF HALF ASIA

TO SIN KING

THIS Creed deserves to rank among the sublimest literary productions of the human mind, from Job to Kant, together with those of the best thinkers of India and China.

Many devout people of the Confucian and Taoist schools, as well as Buddhists, recite it daily just as Christians sing a choice hymn.

It states the solid fundamental principles of religion which commend themselves, not merely to the majority of Asiatics, but also to the majority of men universally. It includes the need of Divine Power to save men, the great At-One-ment, Divine Inspiration, Divinest Miracles, past, present and to come, and Immortality.

When this best Eastern thought is united to the best Western thought, whatever may be deficient in definition in either singly, may meet the approval of that conscience which God has given to mankind collectively.

267

The Creed is as follows :—

Hail self-existent Illuminator, Who in exercising deepest Wisdom seest the unreality of all that is reached by the five senses, and canst save from all troubles and dangers.

O Sariputra (the Divine Seed ?), the Manifested is not different from the Eternal, and the Eternal is not different from the Manifested. Thought and Action are also thus mutually related.

The Divine Seed (?) is the Eternal in all laws of the Universe. He was never born, nor will ever die. (See Living Seed, p. 167.)

He is neither clean nor unclean, is neither added to nor subtracted from. He is without sorrow, and will not perish. He is without acquired Wisdom, because he has received none.

The Illuminators depending on this Eternal Wisdom are without anxiety. Having no anxiety, they have no fear and are far from impossible dreams and thoughts. They are eventually immortals.

All the Illumined past, present, and to come, depending on this Divine Wisdom, obtain the Highest Wisdom.

Therefore know that this Divine Wisdom is a great Divine Magic, a great brilliant magic, the greatest magic, and a magic without a peer.

It can deliver you from all kinds of troubles. This is a real truth without any falsehood.   There-

fore in repeating this magic Incantation, sum up
and say—

> Praise, Praise,
> Praise God.
> Praise His eternal wisdom (Law)
> Praise the students of this Law
>   The Illumined !

[Translated from the Buddhist Tripitaka, Nanjio's
Catalogue, No. 20.]

INDEX

———•———

271

Printed by
MORRISON & GIBB LIMITED
Edinburgh

A GREAT ENCYCLOPÆDIA.

VOLUMES ONE AND TWO   NOW READY

ENCYCLOPÆDIA

OF

RELIGION AND ETHICS

EDITED BY

Dr. JAMES HASTINGS.

THE purpose of this Encyclopædia is to give a complete account of Religion and Ethics so far as they are known. It will contain articles on every separate religious belief and practice, and on every ethical or philosophical idea and custom. Persons and places that have contributed to the history of religion and morals will also be described.

The Encyclopædia will cover a distinct department of knowledge. It is the department which has always exercised the greatest influence over men's lives, and its interest at least, if not its influence, is probably greater at the present time than ever. Within the scope of 'Religion and Ethics' come all the questions that are most keenly debated in PSYCHOLOGY and in SOCIALISM, while the title will be used to embrace the whole of THEOLOGY and PHILOSOPHY. Ethics and Morality will be handled as thoroughly as religion.

Some Prominent Contributors.

In BUDDHISM — Profs. Rhys Davids, Geden, Cabaton, de la Vallée Poussin, Vidyabhusana ; Lieut.-Col. Wadedll.

In the RELIGION OF CHINA AND JAPAN—Sir E. M. Satow, Sir Walter Hillier, Profs. Anesaki, Chamberlain, de Groot, Lloyd, Revon, Takakusu.

In the RELIGION OF INDIA—Sir C. J. Lyall, Sir H. H. Risley, Col. Sir R. C. Temple, Bart., Major P. R. Gurdon, Profs. Deussen, Garbe, Jacobi, Macdonell.

It is estimated that the work will be completed in Ten Volumes of about 900 pages each, size $11\frac{1}{2}''$ by $9''$.

VOLUMES ONE AND TWO NOW READY.

Price, per vol., Cloth Binding, 28s. net.	Each Volume may be had in Twelve Monthly Parts,
and in Half-Morocco, . . . 34s. net.	Price 2s. 6d. net each Part.

VOLUME THREE IN THE PRESS.

THE
PHILOSOPHY OF THE UPANISHADS.
THE RELIGION AND PHILOSOPHY OF INDIA.
By Prof. P. DEUSSEN,
University of Kiel.

Translated by Prof. A. S. GEDEN, M.A.   8vo, **10s. 6d.**

'A volume of extraordinary ability. Professor Deussen is easily first in this study at the present day. It is such an introduction to the study of the religion and philosophy of India as English readers have long been seeking. To every Indian Brahman to-day the Upanishads are what the New Testament is to the Christian.'—Dr. HASTINGS, in the *Expository Times*.

BUDDHA AND BUDDHISM.
By ARTHUR LILLIE.   3s.

'Mr. Lillie has succeeded in clearly and lucidly mapping out the main broad facts of this fascinating religion.'—*Oxford Review*.

'His book is a solid performance, showing much industry and scholarship, and his presentation of Buddha and his message of peace, charity, and universal benevolence is both discriminating and sympathetic, and deserves hearty welcome.'—*Indian Review*.

MUHAMMAD AND HIS POWER.
By P. DE LACY JOHNSTONE, M.A.   3s.

'Every page of his brilliant, confident narrative reveals the man who knows.'—*Expository Times*.

'Gives in a moderate compass a thoroughly good popular account of Muhammad's career and influence.'—*Guardian*.

ROUSSEAU AND NATURALISM IN
LIFE AND THOUGHT.
By Prof. W. H. HUDSON, M.A.   3s.

'Prof. Hudson has skilfully done the difficult work of writing a short account of Rousseau. His book is well proportioned, clear, and eminently readable. He does full justice to the literary power of his subject, and he expounds his chief doctrines—political, educational, and religious—with admirable clearness and conciseness.'—*Manchester Guardian*.

NOW READY.

Crown quarto, 1008 Pages, with Four Maps, price 20s. net; or in Half-Leather Binding, 25s. net.

DICTIONARY OF THE BIBLE.

COMPLETE IN ONE VOLUME.

EDITED BY

JAMES HASTINGS, D.D.

This Dictionary is entirely distinct from the Five - Volume Dictionary.

It is complete in ONE Volume.

The Articles are all new.

It is not based on any other Dictionary, but is a wholly new and original Work.

Every Article is signed by the Author. This is the first time that all the Articles in a single-volume Dictionary of the Bible have been committed to Specialists and bear their signatures, as in the largest Dictionaries.

Prospectus, with Specimen Page and List of Authors, post free on application.

FROM PRESS NOTICES.

'A very fine achievement, worthy to stand beside his larger Dictionaries, and by far the most scholarly yet produced in one volume in English-speaking countries, perhaps it may be said in the world.'—*Christian World.*

'The names of the editor and assistants alone are guarantees for the thoroughness with which everything that belongs to the production of a dictionary is attended to, and nothing could surpass the care, clearness, and accuracy which characterise the work from beginning to end.'—*Churchman.*

'To produce in a single volume a Dictionary of the Bible sufficiently ample in its scope and plan, abreast of present scholarship, not too elementary to be of use to students and ministers, and not too technical and scholastic in its method for an ordinary reader is, as will be readily understood, an extremely difficult undertaking. So far as our examination of it has gone, it has been admirably accomplished.'—*Methodist Recorder.*

'An exceedingly valuable and comprehensive work.'—*Record.*

'The work is able, scholarly, and of a thoroughly trustworthy kind. The editor has been able to enlist the foremost scholars of our time. We must call attention to the careful and masterly sub-editing. It is as near perfection as is possible for man to attain.'—*Aberdeen Free Press.*

'Thoroughly abreast of present-day knowledge. For presentation and library purposes the book outstrips all its rivals, and its closely packed pages are a perfect mine for teachers and ministers.'—*Sunday School Chronicle.*

'No pains have been spared to make the book thoroughly reliable and up to date.'—*Scotsman.*

'Abundance of sound learning in a small compass.'—*Times.*

HANDBOOKS FOR BIBLE CLASSES AND PRIVATE STUDENTS.

EDITED BY

PRINCIPAL A. WHYTE, D.D., AND JOHN KELMAN, D.D.

'I name specially the admirable Handbooks for Bible Classes issued by T. & T. Clark of Edinburgh. They are very cheap, and among them are some books unsurpassed in their kind.'—Sir W. ROBERTSON NICOLL in *The British Weekly.*

COMMENTARIES—

Principal MARCUS DODS, D.D. **Genesis.** 2s.

JAMES MACGREGOR, D.D. **Exodus.** 2 Vols. 2s. each.

Principal DOUGLAS, D.D. **Joshua.** 1s. 6d. **Judges.** 1s. 3d.

Professor J. G. MURPHY, LL.D. **Chronicles.** 1s. 6d.

Rev. JAMES AITKEN, M.A. **The Book of Job.** 1s. 6d.

Principal MARCUS DODS, D.D. **Haggai, Zechariah, Malachi.** 2s.

Principal DOUGLAS, D.D. **Obadiah to Zephaniah.** 1s. 6d.

Rev. EDWARD E. ANDERSON, M.A. **St. Matthew's Gospel.** 2s. 6d.

Principal T. M. LINDSAY, D.D. **Mark.** 2s. 6d.

Principal T. M. LINDSAY, D.D. **St. Luke.** 2 Vols. 3s. 3d. (Vol. I., 2s. ; Vol. II., 1s. 3d.)

GEORGE REITH, D.D. **St. John.** 2 Vols. 2s. each.

Principal T. M. LINDSAY, D.D. **Acts.** 2 Vols. 1s. 6d. each.

Principal BROWN, D.D. **Romans.** 2s.

JAMES MACGREGOR, D.D. **Galatians.** 1s. 6d.

Professor J. S. CANDLISH, D.D. **Ephesians.** 1s. 6d.

Professor A. B. DAVIDSON, D.D. **Hebrews.** 2s. 6d.

Rev. J. P. LILLEY, D.D. **The Pastoral Epistles.** 2s. 6d.

GENERAL SUBJECTS—

Professor JAMES STALKER, D.D.
The Life of Christ. 1s. 6d.
The Life of St. Paul. 1s. 6d.
(*Large-type Editions,* 3s. 6d. *each.*)

ALEXANDER WHYTE, D.D.
The Shorter Catechism. 2s. 6d.

Professor J. S. CANDLISH, D.D.
The Christian Sacraments. 1s. 6d.
The Christian Doctrine of God. 1s. 6d.
The Work of the Holy Spirit. 1s. 6d.
The Biblical Doctrine of Sin. 1s. 6d.

NORMAN L. WALKER, D.D.
Scottish Church History. 1s. 6d.

Rev. W. D. THOMSON, M.A.
The Christian Miracles and the Conclusions of Science. 2s.

GEORGE SMITH, LL.D., F.R.G.S., C.I.E.
History of Christian Missions. 2s. 6d.

ARCHIBALD HENDERSON, D.D.
Palestine: Its Historical Geography. *With Maps.* 2s. 6d.

Principal T. M. LINDSAY, D.D.
The Reformation. 2s.

REV. JOHN MACPHERSON, M.A.
The Sum of Saving Knowledge. 1s. 6d.
The Confession of Faith.
Presbyterianism. 1s. 6d.

Professor BINNIE, D.D.
The Church. 1s. 6d.

Professor T. B. KILPATRICK, D.D.
Butler's Three Sermons on Human Nature. 1s. 6d.

President HAMILTON, D.D.
History of the Irish Presbyterian Church. 2s.

Rev. W. SCRYMGEOUR, M.A.
Lessons on the Life of Christ. 2s. 6d.

A. TAYLOR INNES, M.A., Advocate.
Church and State. 3s.

Rev. J. FEATHER.
The Last of the Prophets—John the Baptist. 2s.

Rev. W. FAIRWEATHER, M.A.
From the Exile to the Advent. 2s.

Professor J. LAIDLAW, D.D.
Foundation Truths of Scripture as to Sin and Salvation. 1s. 6d.

Rev. L. A. MUIRHEAD, D.D.
The Times of Christ. 2s.

Rev. J. P. LILLEY, D.D.
The Principles of Protestantism. 2s. 6d.

Rev. J. STRACHAN, M.A.
Hebrew Ideals. 2 Vols. 2s. each (or the 2 Vols. bound in One, 3s. net).

Rev. D. M. ROSS, D.D.
The Teaching of Jesus. 2s.

Prof. J. DICK FLEMING, B.D.
Israel's Golden Age. 1s. 6d.

Rev. W. BEVERIDGE, M.A.
Makers of the Scottish Church. 2s.